SS PEIPER

SS PEIPER

BATTLE COMMANDER SS LEIBSTANDARTE ADOLF HITLER

by
Charles Whiting

Pen & Sword
MILITARY

First published in Great Britain in 1986 by
Leo Cooper in association with Secker and Warburg Ltd

Republished in this revised edition in 1999
and reprinted in 2012 by
PEN & SWORD MILITARY
An imprint of
Pen & Sword Books Ltd
47 Church Street
Barnsley
South Yorkshire
S70 2AS

Copyright © Charles Whiting 1986, 1999, 2012

ISBN 978 1 84884 861 0

The right of Charles Whiting to be identified as Author
of this work has been asserted by him in accordance with the
Copyright, Designs and Patents Act 1988.

Printed and bound in England
By CPI Group (UK) Ltd, Croydon, CR0 4YY

Pen & Sword Books Ltd incorporates the Imprints of Pen & Sword Aviation,
Pen & Sword Family History, Pen & Sword Maritime, Pen & Sword Military,
Pen & Sword Discovery, Wharncliffe Local History, Wharncliffe True Crime,
Wharncliffe Transport, Pen & Sword Select, Pen & Sword Military Classics,
Leo Cooper, The Praetorian Press, Remember When,
Seaforth Publishing and Frontline Publishing

For a complete list of Pen & Sword titles please contact
PEN & SWORD BOOKS LIMITED
47 Church Street, Barnsley, South Yorkshire, S70 2AS, England
E-mail: enquiries@pen-and-sword.co.uk
Website: www.pen-and-sword.co.uk

CONTENTS

Introduction   ix

PART I: Baptism of Blood
One   3
Two   6
Three   11
Four   13
Five   19
Six   25
Seven   28
Eight   31
Nine   38

PART II: The Crime
One   43
Two   49
Three   53
Four   57
Five   59
Six   68
Seven   74
Eight   81
Nine   85
Ten   89

PART III: The Reckoning
One   95
Two   102

Three   107
Four   113
Five   119

PART IV: Trial at Dachau
One   129
Two   137
Three   152
Four   158

PART V: The Old Man of Traves
One   167
Two   171
Three   174
Four   177
Five   180

Envoi   185

Appendix The Arrest of Jochen Peiper 187

Index   193

'We are all ready to be savage in some cause. The difference between a good man and a bad one is the choice of the cause.'

William James

INTRODUCTION

'I cannot tell how the truth may be;
I say the tale as 'twas said to me'.
                                    Walter Scott.

'I swear to you, Adolf Hitler, as Führer and Reich Chancellor, loyalty and bravery. I vow to you, and those you have named to command me, obedience unto death. So help me God.'

This was the oath that an intense, twenty-year-old German swore one January morning in the year 1935. Standing rigidly to attention, right hand raised, he faced the skull-and-crossbones banner and pledged himself for life to the new master of Germany's destiny. That morning in Brunswick, fifty years ago, Jochen Peiper pledged himself to the new Führer and thus became a member of a select force: Hitler's new praetorian guard *SS Leibstandarte Adolf Hitler.* His fate had been sealed.

He was a slight young man, dwarfed by the other cadets solemnly intoning the oath; for they had all been picked, like British guardsmen, on account of their height and physique. His hair was dark and slick and slightly longer than was customary at the time. The face was lean with a strong jaw and steady, well-set eyes. The mouth was tight and wilful, as if its owner had to keep a tight rein on his emotions.

It was the kind of face which the German novelist, Ernst Juenger, had envisaged when he described the ideal German soldier of the future: 'A new man, the storm trooper, the elite of Central Europe. A completely new race, cunning, strong and packed with purpose . . . battle-proven, merciless both to himself and others.' One day Cadet Jochen Peiper, who had just entered the ranks of the Black Guards, the *Waffen SS,* would be all of that, and more!

Yet he was no fanatic, in spite of what the world Press would write of him when he became notorious. He was highly intelligent and well-read, unlike most of his contemporaries; in the main they were blond farmers' sons from the north. He spoke French and German fluently (in his old age and self-imposed exile he would earn his living translating books). He had society connections. He was charming, courteous and, unusual for a German, he had, in Anglo-Saxon eyes, that saving grace of having a sense of humour, though, as we will see, his humour sometimes took macabre, almost suicidal forms.

Right from the start, he was regarded as arrogant in SS circles. '*Arrogantes Schwein!*' was the last comment that his future commander, General Sepp Dietrich, would ever make about Peiper. He did not join the Nazi Party like most of his contemporaries. During his cadet training he refused to wear uniform off-duty, whenever it was possible, so that he did not have to salute the 'golden pheasants', the fat pompous Party officials in their gold-braided uniforms. Later, when he commanded his own unit during the war, he went his own way, resolving his own problems without consulting his superiors. Because he was a brilliant tactician and succeeded so often, he got away with it. Interrogating Peiper just after his capture, US Major Ken Hechler found him to be extremely proud of his command, but highly contemptuous of other outfits, quick to make derogatory remarks about their commanders and their performance in battle. For Jochen Peiper there was only one outfit of any value – *Die Leibstandarte Adolf Hitler!*

In short, he was keen, ambitious, pushy, contemptuous of older officers and civilians, especially if they were in authority, and he was eager for rank, command *and glory*! In the Second World War, he got all three quickly.

Mentioned in the *Wehrmacht* war reports several times, featured on the covers of Party magazines, presented with the Knight's Cross and the two further classes of that award, he rose quickly up the ladder of promotion. He fought throughout the war on virtually every front without a single serious scratch; he was a regimental colonel at twenty-seven – the youngest in the *Waffen SS*. Undoubtedly he would have become a general by the time he was thirty, but that wasn't to be. By then Germany had lost the war and the world no longer needed people like *Obersturmbannführer der Waffen SS* Jochen Peiper. His bright comet had made its brief flight across the heavens. Now it was to fall to earth with a resounding, terrible crash.

The Armed SS, 'the scourge of Europe', as it has been called, to which the young colonel belonged for ten years, was going to have to pay a heavy price for its brief moment of military glory. But none of the many thousands of SS officers who survived the war paid a higher price than Peiper. He would live under sentence of death by hanging for nearly five years. When the heavy footsteps sounded every evening in the corridor outside his cell door, he would never know whether they had come to escort him to the gallows or merely to bring him his supper. Four times his interrogators took him out to mock hangings and, finally, when the torture was over and he has been reprieved, he would serve another seven years in prison.

Even after his release Peiper was not left in peace. Time and again his past caught up with him and he was forced to flee from job to job. In the end, he had enough; he went into voluntary exile in a remote French village. For five years he led a solitary existence – 'the happiest time of my whole life' – until he reckoned that the world had at last forgotten him and his crime. It hadn't!

One July, thirty years almost to the day since he had been sentenced to death, his murderers came for him in the night. At the age of sixty-one, alone save for his two pet dogs and armed with an ancient revolver and a hunting rifle, he fought them off. But the two Molotov cocktails they flung at his home did their work well. The wooden house in the forest burst into flames and Jochen Peiper died in the resultant holocaust, some said fittingly so. Thus died the last victim of a massacre which had taken place nearly three and a half decades before. The wheel had come the full circle.

What had been his crime? Officially he was accused in 1945 of being the commander of a military force which had cold-bloodedly killed some eighty unarmed US Army prisoners-of-war on 17 December, 1944, at the crossroads in the little Belgian hamlet of Baugnez during the Battle of the Bulge. It was the greatest massacre of Allied troops in the West during the Second World War and, as the first survivors escaped to the nearby town of Malmédy, the incident was given the name of 'the Malmédy Massacre'. The incident became an international legal and political issue, a *cause celèbre* of the forties and fifties, occupying the minds not only of soldiers, lawyers and judges, but also of writers, journalists, film-makers, archbishops, even the President of the United States himself.

In the years to come the handsome young SS colonel in a black leather jacket, Knight's Cross at his neck, would become the movie-goer's archetypal image of the SS officer, as portrayed, for instance, by Robert Shaw in the movie account of the Battle of the Bulge. Peiper's face under the peaked cap with its silver death's head badge seemed to symbolize the power and the terror of Nazi Germany.

Officially, Jochen Peiper was guilty. Whatever happened that Sunday in December, 1944, was indirectly but undoubtedly his responsibility. In the final analysis the military commander is responsible for the actions of his men, even though, in this case, they numbered five thousand and were spread out over many miles, some of them engaged in one of the most confused battles of the Second World War. Another commander would have refused to have accepted responsibility. SS General Lammerding of the 2nd SS Panzer Division, whose men massacred nearly four hundred civilians at the French village of Oradour-sur-Glane, for example, refused to accept the overall responsibility for the actions of his men – and got away with it. Peiper was different. That fatal arrogance of his ensured that he would take the guilt upon himself, although he was at least a dozen miles away when whatever happened at the crossroads took place.

But what *did* happen there? Years later, the man who should know, for after all he had suffered most as a result, could laugh in that bitter, cynical manner of his and answer the author's question by saying: '*Malmédy!* Who knows and who cares any more? No one – *no one* – will ever sort out the mess now! Too many lies have been told these last twenty-five years or so.' Yet even then, when passions were still aroused and tempers violent, there were some Americans who refused to believe that Peiper was guilty. Some of the soldiers who took up his case risked their military careers and spent their own money to prove that an injustice had been done to Peiper; that the evidence presented against him at his trial was either false or had been obtained under duress, even torture. Twenty-five years after he had been sentenced to death, the chief prosecutor who had been instrumental in having Peiper sentenced, and who, prior to the trial, had indicated that he didn't think Peiper was guilty, spoke of him as 'a fine gentleman' and wrote to him as 'Dear Colonel Peiper'.

In essence Jochen Peiper never really had a chance to escape the trap prepared for him at birth. Born the son of an ex-officer of the Old Imperial Army, who regarded the Weimar Republic as having been created by the men who had stabbed the Army in back during the First World War, he had been brought up in the old Prussian tradition of self-discipline and self-sacrifice. He came to manhood at a time when the new Party bosses knew exactly how to manipulate those virtues for their own political ends. Peiper fell for the party line hook, line and sinker. Filled with the new spirit of hope that Hitler gave the idealistic youth of the time, he marched to war believing in the cause and Nazi Germany's manifest destiny and prepared to sacrifice his young life for it. Instead he became a hero.

Just as time and fate had selected him for a hero, time and fate also selected him to become a victim of the war Germany had lost. In battle he had never been coward; he had always sought the boldest, most impossible missions for himself. Where more sensible officers had hesitated, he had dashed forward, eager to accept any sacrifice for the sake of his country, his cause, his command. Now, in defeat, he still could not learn to become a coward, as so many of his former comrades did. Defeat, even when he was faced with overwhelming odds, was another battle to be fought. The result was predictable. Because Peiper would not be reasonable, the whole weight of the US Army was brought to bear against him and, of course, 'Uncle Sam' won.

What happened at the trial of Jochen Peiper was no advertisement for either American justice or democracy, save for the actions of those few brave Americans who stood up for Peiper. Later it would be shown that the evidence against him had been obtained from his men by threats, promises, beatings and sometimes outright torture. But in the years that were to follow, it no longer mattered. Jochen Peiper had been branded as a war criminal and the rest of his life was ruined. Thus perhaps in the end when his killers came for him he was glad to accept his death, glad that at last it was all over. Who knows? Peiper was never a very talkative man.

This, then, is the story of SS Peiper, whose fate was typical of a German of his class, age, and time – first war hero and then war criminal. It is the tale of a man whose sentence of death was finally carried out thirty years after it had been passed. And if there is any lesson to be learned from SS Peiper's harsh, perhaps even tragic, life it is this: *On this earth there is no hiding place save in the grave itself.*

PART I

Baptism of Blood

'Heute gehört uns Deutschland und morgen die
ganze Welt!'*

The Nazi Horst Wessel Song

* Today Germany belongs to us, tomorrow the whole world.

ONE

The little French ironmonger was curious. The customer had been coming to his shop for quite a while now to buy nails, wire, screws, and the like. Yet he still did not know who he was and his provincial curiosity was aroused. Where did the man come from and what was he doing in Vesoul? In the last few years a lot of new industry had come to the French town, set deep down in the valley at the foot of the Vosges. The town had spread and spread until the factories had begun to climb the steep hillsides. With the new industry had come the foreigners and this man was obviously a foreigner. His French was rapid and correct, perhaps too correct, but he was a foreigner all the same. With that hard hawklike face, surmounted by white hair, worn unfashionably long, he was obviously no humble Spanish immigrant or 'Macaroni'. The customer radiated a sense of authority in spite of his casual, inexpensive clothes. Could he be one of those calculating Dutchmen who counted every *sou* three times over? Or perhaps an Englishman, very polite in their bumbling way, but as arrogant as they had always been? He knew there were some of them living locally in their holiday homes. Or a German? There were plenty of them too, spending their summers in their 'bungalows' and 'villas', as they always called their wooden shacks in the Vosges – pudgy, moneyed men, who drove their fat Mercedes as if they were tanks.

But if this customer who so intrigued him was German, he didn't look it. There was nothing soft about this man. He was old admittedly and his shirt collar seemed too big for him, but his eyes still flashed fire and that lean, hard face had something cynical about it, as if he had long seen through his fellow men.

The ironmonger started to ask questions, but it was not just provincial noseyness which prompted him to do so. The ironmonger was politically active. In spite of being a shop-owner and therefore a *bourgeois*, he subscribed to that creed which was going to change the world one day. *He was a communist!*

In Traves, a straggle of houses on a hill, a church, a store-cum-post-office, some twelve kilometres to the east of Vesoul, the old man they called *L'Allemand* dreamed his days away. Out there in his wooden house in the forest on the banks of the River Saône, he lived a quiet life. There were other Germans living there, too, at least in the summer. But the old German, his wife and family, when they were there, kept to themselves. They had their dogs, Timm and Tamm; they had their nesting boxes and feeding troughs for the birds, and they had their dreams.

'Here,' his son said later, when it was all over, 'he enjoyed that security and peace he had always dreamed about in the death cell. Then he had always thought it impossible that one day he would possess a house on his own grounds under the trees. Now he had it – a dream come true.'

Of course he did a little work, too. He had to, in order to support himself and his wife, who was constantly ill. Since he had finally gone into exile here four years earlier, he had earned a modest living translating books on military subjects from English into German. But he tried to work out of doors as much as possible. Followed by his faithful dog, Timm, he sawed wood for his open fire, did his washing, picked mushrooms, trying to forget the past, feeling that his dog was 'more of a brother to me than many of those two-legged creatures who have done so much harm to me'.

Of an evening he would sit in front of his crackling wood fire, drinking his favourite 'Earl Grey' tea, smoking his pipe, and listening to classical music. Now his motto was, 'Yesterday is past, tomorrow does not exist, *today* is important'.

Here in this 'paradise', as he called it, although it was only a modest' wooden house situated at the edge of a dull French hamlet of 365 souls, he had found peace at last. In one of the last letters he wrote to his wife in Munich, he said, 'Civilization does not release its children untouched. All the same it is unbelievably beautiful here, in spite of the remains of the chains which, invisible as they are, one still drags around with one. From here everything falls into perspective. . . . On this island everything is positive. Hopefuly it will tolerate us a while longer and be available for other shipwrecked people after us.'

But that was not to be. The 'island' would tolerate the old German no longer. The inquiries of the little ironmonger in Vesoul were progressing apace. *L'Allemand* lived in Traves all the year round, he had found out, unlike the other foreigners, who spent only their holidays there. He worked too. From fellow communists in the postal service he had learned that *L'Allemand* received many letters from abroad, from Germany, England, even the United States. He telephoned a great deal and his telephone conversations always seemed to be about the war.

Then the busy ironmonger made his most important discovery of all. Somehow or other he obtained possession of the French edition of the *Braunes Buch* (the Brown Book), published by the state publishing company of the German Democratic Republic. This publication listed all alleged former war criminals, living or working in West Germany. He ran his finger down the names until he came to the one he sought:

'PEIPER, JOACHIM
*avant 1945: Oberstürmbannfuhrer SS (no 132 496); membre des Waffen SS avec le même grade; responsable de la destrucion par le feu de la localité de Boves en Italie, dont il donna l'ordre au titre de commandant d'un regiment de blindes de la division blindée SS 'Leibstandarte Adolf Hitler' responsable de l'assassinat de 71 prisonniers de guerre americains désarmés au sud de Malmédy, au mois de Decembre 1944.
après 1945: condamné à mort par un tribunal militaire americain, peine commuée plus tard en 25 ans de reclusion, rémis en liberté en 1956; il a travaillé aux entreprises Porsche; puis, il est devenu chef de publicité d'un magasin de vente de Volkswagen à Reutlingen.'*

The ironmonger sat back in triumph. *He had him!* He had landed a really big fish! The old German in Traves was a colonel of the SS. More, he had been convicted of two atrocities, the burning of the Italian village of Boves in 1943 and the cold-blooded shooting of American prisoners-of-war at Malmédy in Belgium a year later.

Now this war criminal, this Joachim Peiper, was living secretly in their midst, in a country which those black guards had terrorized back in the early '40s, alive thirty years after the Americans had condemned him to death. Something had to be done about it. The comrades in Paris had to be informed; it was a public scandal and an insult to France and those brave comrades of the *Resistance* who still survived. The ironmonger reached for his telephone and began to dial a Paris number. Now the wheels began to turn. A murder was going to be arranged.

TWO

Berlin 1933

Since 30 January a new leader had commanded the destiny of Germany – Adolf Hitler. The pimps, the pederasts, the poofs had almost vanished, as had the communists, and soon the socialists. It was no longer Christopher Isherwood's Berlin. A fresh wind blew in the city on the River Spree.

Of course, the new *Prominenz* were as perverted as the old. Captain Roehm, the commander of the SA, could still enjoy his pretty boys. Goering painted his nails and rouged his cheeks, and occasionally sniffed his 'coke' from a bejewelled container. Goebbels, the club-footed 'poison dwarf' (as he was called behind his back on account of his stature and vitriolic tongue), could run a whole stable of beautiful mistresses. Even the Führer himself was not blameless.

But for the man in the street Hitler brought hope and the prospect of a brighter future after years of decline, poverty, and impotence. '*Brot und Arbeit*' (bread and work) was his slogan and he already seemed to be beginning to realize that bold promise made to a nation with six million of its citizens out of work. For eighteen-year old Joachim (he preferred to be called 'Jochen' rather than use his given name which was of biblical origin) Peiper it was an exciting time to set out into the world.

Born on 30 January, 1915, a significant date,* he was the son of Captain Waldemar Peiper. His father had disdained the mass slaughter of the trenches in the First World War. Instead he had fought in the guerrilla campaign in East Africa, where a small German force had held down a much superior Allied force for years. There he had been severely wounded and sent back to the Reich to experience the shame

* The Kaiser's birthday and the date of Hitler's takeover.

of defeat. Peiper, therefore, came from a home where the Army and patriotism loomed large. Now that Army, which had been reduced to exactly 100,000 men by order of the victorious Allies, would undoubtedly come into its own again. Hitler had already publicly repudiated the *Versaillesdiktat* and it was obvious that he would expand the Army and there would be a need for new blood. Jochen Peiper would inevitably follow in his father's footsteps and become an Army officer.

But there was one catch. Although highly intelligent and very articulate, Peiper had slacked at his high school, the *Goethe Ober-realschule*, with the result that he now failed the *Abitur*. Without the 'Abi' as the boys called it, the doors to university, technical college or an Army officer's career were barred to him.

However, he had something up his sleeve. He was already a member of the Hitler Youth, so now he joined Berlin's *SS Reitersturm*, the SS cavalry, which had been set up by the head of the SS, Himmler, in an effort to attract socially respectable elements to the SS. Indeed the Berlin squadron numbered two Hohenzollern princes in its ranks.

Peiper mixed well with those of gentle birth attracted to the new formation, but he wanted more than decorous gallops in the *Spreewald* and cultivated chats about the cosmos. He wanted adventure, such as his father had found in East Africa, but the Army wouldn't have him. Thus it was that he volunteered for the SS.

On 17 February, 1934, he wrote to the headquarters of SS District East, applying for membership of the SS and proclaiming his intention of making the SS his career as an officer. His application fell into the hands of Sepp Dietrich, simultaneously head of the District and commander of the infant *Leibstandarte Adolf Hitler*.

The burly ex-tank sergeant, who would one day share Peiper's imprisonment, liked the tone of the letter. He forwarded Peiper's name for training. But many other young Germans were making similar applications to join this elite force which formed the Führer's own bodyguard. The newsreels were full of them, forming a triple cordon around the Reich Chancellery and fulfilling guard functions whenever the Führer was in the capital. Soon the sight of these black-clad giants with their white belts and cross-straps would become familiar to people all over the world. To many, indeed, the *Leibstandarte* seemed to symbolize the brutal efficiency of the new régime in Germany.

Finally, in January, 1935, Peiper was called to the *SS Junkerschule* in Brunswick for his admission examination prior to training at the SS cadet school for a regular officer's career in the SS. The doctors thought him rather on the small size for the SS and not as physically well-built as most of the candidates, but he was fit and alert and highly intelligent. He was also examined by SS psychiatrists who found him egocentric and mistrustful of others. His chronic efforts to impress others with his 'connections', gained through the Berlin *Reitersturm*, were also noted by the doctors. In their appraisal, dated 4 April, 1935, they summed the twenty-year-old would-be SS officer up as having a 'strong will and inclined to realize that will in quick impulsive thrusts'. Little did those doctors realize that it was just those qualities which were going to make Jochen Peiper one of the most outstanding young commanders of the Second World War.

In spite of the fact that the *Leibstandarte* was generally regarded as a guards battalion, intended only for ceremonial duties, drilled to the standards of the British Brigade of Guards – indeed, they nicknamed themselves the 'asphalt soldiers' because they were always goose-stepping down the asphalt roads of Berlin – the training of future officers for this formation was radically different from that of the traditional army. At Brunswick the emphasis was laid on developing, not a wooden-minded martinet obsessed with drill and regulations, but an independent, flexible officer, who could lead his men from the front. Emphasis was placed on physical fitness and endurance in adversity. Field craft played a major role. Training was realistic, with live ammunition being used instead of blanks as was the custom with the regular army. They were given shovels, told to dig in and then a platoon of tanks was driven over their foxholes. It was just too bad for the cadet who had not dug deep enough. It was also recorded that cadets were given grenades to place on their helmets. When the grenade was balanced, the instructor retired to a safe distance and ordered the cadet to pull the pin and stand rigidly to attention. Usually there was no damage if the cadet maintained absolute stillness and let the explosion dissipate itself above his steel-clad head. If he became rattled, however, and let the grenade fall. . . .

The man in charge of all SS training, General Berger, known behind his back as the 'Duke of Swabia', aimed at creating a formation which would not be thrown into battle, as had been the case in the First World War, to be slaughtered like cattle by enemy machine-guns. Instead the SS-man would be the modern soldier, as envisaged by Liddell Hart, 'the hunter-poacher-athlete' type. He would be an individualist who knew how to look after himself and who would not throw away his life purposelessly.

There was one other aspect of the training in Brunswick – ideological indoctrination given to these budding officers. Much of it was heavy-handed stuff – dreary dissertations on old 'Germanic' history, designed to glorify the 'Aryan' race, whatever that was; confused rural-racial twaddle about '*Blut und Boden*' and such like, which was dear to *Reichführer* Himmler's pedantic, schoolmaster's heart. But some of it rubbed off. The emphasis on struggle and hardness to one's self – and to the enemy. As Himmler expressed it in a speech to high-ranking SS officers during the war: 'We must be honourable, decent, loyal and comradely to bearers of our own blood, *but to no one else*'.

One of those pre-war officer cadets, Ernst Gunther Kraetschmer, remembers that the 'rules of Germanness were not read out; one learned them by leaps from ten-metre towers and by the most severe training on the exercise grounds'.

Swiftly the months passed, Peiper growing ever more aware that he was destined for an elite formation which owed its loyalty not to the state, but to the ruler of that state, Adolf Hitler. Once he had graduated, he would be at the centre of things, where the decisions were made, *next to the Führer*. It was an exciting prospect for an ambitious young man. In early 1936 he graduated, and was sent on the standard platoon leader's course at the training installation at Dachau. Two months later, on 20 April, 1936, he was commissioned *SS-Untersturmbannführer* – another significant date, Hitler's birthday. Many years later Peiper was to regret that he had not been at the Führer's side on his last birthday. Then he would have died in the capital, defending Hitler to the last, and would never have had to suffer the shame of what was to come after the war.

Almost immediately he was posted to the *Leibstandarte*, in which he was to serve for the rest of his military career, with one significant exception. Here he spent the next two years, in that highly charged atmosphere around Hitler. The young soldiers of the Führer's personal guard certainly took their duties very seriously. Gerd Bremer, then a second-lieutenant, who ended the war as a 26-year-old commander of a regiment in the 'Hitler Youth' Division, recalled years later just how much the SS motto – 'My Loyalty is My Honour'– meant to the young soldiers: 'One night I was on guard duty in charge of Hitler's personal security. It was customary to post a soldier just outside Hitler's personal quarters, with his pistol already drawn. On this particular night Hitler could not sleep. He came out of his quarters at about three in the morning and found one of my young soldiers asleep at a desk, the pistol lying in front of him. Hitler didn't wake the man; after all the place swarmed with police and guards and he knew he was well protected. Instead he took the man's pistol and called me to him the following morning. I expected a terrific bollocking. But all I got was the pistol and the gentle advice to see my men got more sleep before they came on duty. Naturally I let the culprit have it, but as Hitler had not wanted any charges pressed, I left it at that. But the young soldier could not get over the shame of having fallen asleep while guarding the Führer himself. That day he took the pistol that Hitler had taken from him and blew his brains out.'

Peiper loved the *Leibstandarte*, but he was not always the easiest of comrades. Another newly commissioned second-lieutenant recalls Peiper as 'reserved and not given to leading any conversation, but well-respected and tipped by most of his comrades to go far in the SS'. One of his first company commanders, himself immensely tall and very tough, thought that Peiper was not as 'physically tough as his men, most of them at that time giants. He was very head-strong, something which would cause him to lose a lot of men in his first actions in Russia later. But he was going places, that was for certain.'

Peiper certainly was. In July, 1938, he was posted on a three-month assignment to the personal staff of *Reichsführer SS* Heinrich Himmler.

THREE

Number Ten Prinz Albrecht Strasse, Berlin, was the most feared and notorious address in the whole of the Third Reich. For twelve long years, before the much vaunted '1,000 Year Reich' finally collapsed, it was here that the victims and opponents of the régime were brought to be interrogated, tortured, and sometimes dispatched in the cellars of the building which had once been, ironically enough, a school of fine arts. Here the bull-necked 'Gestapo' Mueller, head of the feared secret police, reigned with fear. Here cynical, clever Reinhard Heydrich, 'the man with the iron heart', as Hitler himself called him, ran the SD, the SS's own security service; and here their chief, Heinrich Himmler, ruled over his ever-growing SS empire.

It is not known whether Peiper, in the first three months of his assignment, was aware of what happened in those cellars into which the poor wretches the Gestapo arrested were 'interrogated' with thumb-screws and rubber clubs. But when the assignment was extended, we can suppose that the astute young officer came to his own conclusions. We know that Himmler took him to visit an early concentration camp and we know that, in an 'SS Family' such as Peiper's would become, with his own brother in one of the 'Death's Head' formations (which were responsible for the camps), and two brothers of his future wife in the SS, he would be able to make an educated guess at what was going on at Number Ten, and in Germany as a whole. But like so many young men of that time, Peiper would have reasoned that 'to make an omelette, you need to crack eggs', to use the German phrase. The 'New Order', which Hitler was creating, could not be achieved without casualties. Yet, surprisingly enough, fanatical adherent to the National Socialist cause as he was, Peiper lacked the basic equipment of a true Nazi.

One day, when reporting to Himmler, the latter noted that Peiper did not wear the swastika tie-pin of a Party member. Slightly astonished, he asked his young adjutant whether he was not a member of the NSDAP. When Peiper replied in the negative, saying that he did not want to join now and receive a high Party number and thus appear as an opportunist who had jumped on the bandwagon after the National Socialists had come to power, Himmler immediately telephoned Martin Bormann. He ordered the Party Secretary to let Peiper have a low Party number as soon as one became vacant through death. But apparently no number ever became vacant. Peiper, later regarded as the epitome of the ruthless National Socialist soldier, thus never joined the Nazi Party.

Now, as the threat of war loomed ever larger, Peiper met his future wife for the first time. In the summer of 1938 he was acting as a courier between Berlin and Gmund-am-Tegernsee, where Himmler had set up his summer headquarters on the banks of the beautiful Bavarian lake. One of Himmler's staff was a tall elegant blonde from Schleswig-Holstein who had been recommended as a secretary to Himmler by no less a person than Frau Heydrich. Lina Heydrich was contemptuous of Himmler and his wife, who, she maintained, wore 'size forty flannel knickers'. She thought her old school-friend Sigurd, a really true Nordic type, would add a little class to the Himmler entourage; and Himmler, small, sallow and definitely non-Aryan-looking himself, preferred to surround himself with tall, blond Nordic types. Thus she was accepted to work for the *Reichsführer* and came into Jochen Peiper's life.

Himmler himself welcomed the love affair. He was always insisting that his officers should marry so that they could 'further the Aryan race'. He himself had two illegitimate children by another of his secretaries, Hedwig Potthast, who became his mistress in 1940. As late as 1944, he was lecturing bachelor Gerd Bremer: 'There will be no more promotion for you, Bremer, or any other of my officers who remains unmarried. I want babies to make up for our losses in Russia, lots of them!' Bremer married soon after.

In due course the Peipers had three children, two girls and a boy, and Himmler was delighted. But the children were doomed to an unhappy childhood and Sigurd Peiper to spend virtually a whole decade of her life without her husband, the wife of a branded war criminal, trying to bring up her children by herself. Indeed, in one of her last letters before she died in 1979 she wrote to her son: 'Looking back at my life now, the course of which seems to me to be more the stuff novels are made of, I often feel that I have been merely a spectator of some kind of tragedy'.

FOUR

Jochen Peiper went to war in September, 1939, not as he had expected at the head of a column of the *Leibstandarte's* tanks, but by courtesy of the *Reichsbahn*, in a train. To his despair, he was kept away from the fighting war. Instead he travelled to Poland in Hitler's own personal train as part of the headquarters staff under the command of a certain Colonel Rommel, who, like Peiper, was champing at the bit. He, too, wanted to be in the fighting. So while the *Leibstandarte* underwent its baptism of blood in Poland as an armoured infantry regiment, suffering higher casualties than any other unit of the army corps to which it was attached, Peiper remained strictly a military tourist, and he didn't like it one bit. Like Rommel, he knew that promotion came rapidly in war, but only if you were with a combat unit. There, battle casualties ensured that an officer could move up the ladder of promotion ten times as swiftly as in peacetime. Peiper was right, of course. In the next three years he would rise from first lieutenant to full colonel. Desperately he pleaded with Himmler to be freed from his duties as first adjutant and return to the *Leibstandarte* before the war ended. Himmler relented and in the middle of the *Sitzkrieg* he was posted back to his parent unit, which was already being refitted and built up to the strength of a reinforced regiment, ready for the great attack on the West.

On 10 May, 1940, the *Wehrmacht* invaded neutral Belgium and Holland. The *Leibstandarte* followed up the initial infantry-airborne attack with a tremendous drive of seventy miles in one day through Holland. It reached Rotterdam just in time to become involved in the last of the fighting there. Here one group of the regiment managed to achieve a kind of dubious fame by seriously wounding General Student, the German airborne commander, two hours after the cease-fire had taken place. After that the SS were never very popular with General Student. Thereafter, the *Leibstandarte* took part in the operations in France, where Peiper experienced his first taste of battle and found it to his liking. He won the Iron Cross, First and Second Class. Himmler was tremendously pleased when he heard of the award. He ordered that two cars 'liberated' in France should be maintained at Hitler's headquarters for the duration of the war for the personal use of Peiper and Max Wuensche, another favourite. Of course, immediately the war ended with a German victory, he intended to replace the two automobiles with German vehicles.

A year later Captain, as he was now, Peiper took part in the high-speed jaunt through Yugoslavia and on into Greece, where Dietrich took the surrender of a whole Greek army on the Corinth Canal and helped to rout the British and Anzac troops sent to help the Greeks. Yet another Dunkirk for the British and another triumph for those bold young men who wore the silver skull-and-crossbones on their caps. Where would their next battle be? Or had the damned Tommies had enough? Would they not now surrender? After all, Germany now dominated the whole of Western Europe from Norway in the north to Greece in the south, and from France in the west to Poland in the east. In this glorious victorious spring of 1941 Adolf Hitler ruled an empire greater than Rome's. But Hitler, who had sworn he would never make the same mistake the Kaiser had made in the First World War of attempting to fight on two fronts – east and west – was now carried away by his own triumphs. The *Wehrmacht* was unbeatable. Had it not broken the might of the Anglo-French Empires in a matter of months? Which army on this earth was capable of stopping it? Self-opinionated, deluded, and surrounded by yes-men, as he was, he gave that fatal order which would destroy Germany and change the face of the world: Soviet Russia was to be attacked.

Four times the *Leibstandarte* would be sent to the Russian front and four times it would return, exhausted, decimated, its men virtually walking skeletons. In the first campaign, in November, 1941, it penetrated six hundred miles into Russia until it was finally stopped on the River Don by the 'Ivans', as the SS called their opponents. The headlong dash across the steppe against the rabble of the demoralized Red Army had come to an end. Now all winter the *Leibstandarte* fought a bitter defensive battle, not only against the Red Army, but against 'General Winter' himself.

Food was in short supply. For weeks on end the men saw no bread and precious little meat; the weekly ration per soldier was 150 grams! With none of the special winter clothing needed for this kind of fighting, the SS fought in temperatures twenty and thirty degrees below zero, where tank engines would not start unless they were kept running every ten minutes through the night and where sights clouded up, due to lack of special Arctic greases, and turrets froze. The men went down like flies with trench-foot and scurvy, a disease unknown in Germany since the Middle Ages. Even in the SS, men started inflicting wounds upon themselves – a rifle bullet fired through a sandbag at the foot in order to prevent the tell-tale-blackened skin of the self-inflicted wound; diesel oil rubbed into the chest to cause an incurable form of skin disease. There were even tales of SS men deserting to the Ivans to escape this killing misery.

It was against this background that Peiper rose to prominence. Now that stubborn will and resourcefulness of his started to pay dividends. Superior command was loose. Dietrich held the reins slack. His only order to his subordinates when they went into battle was: 'Now be sure and bring back my boys.' He left the fighting to young officers such as Peiper, and Peiper seized the opportunity with both hands. Time and again he acted without orders, rising swiftly from second-in-command of a company to company commander, then battalion commander. He demanded much of his soldiers. His first company commander, H. Frey, noted that in his initial action in Russia, 'he lost a lot of his men wounded due to his dash and failure to make full use of the tactical situation'. But they admired him all the same. For he was not just a glory hunter who let his men win his 'tin', as they called the decorations handed out by the basketful. Peiper led from the front. Once, when his group was attacked by the feared T-34 tanks, he seized a rifle grenade from a *panzergrenadier* and went stalking one of the 30-ton monsters himself. He let the tank come within twenty metres of him before coolly taking aim and lobbing the grenade at the tank, which ground to a halt in a violent burst of flame. Tossing the rifle back to its owner, he cried, 'That should do for the close-combat badge, eh boys!'

But he paid the price for his steady rise to prominence. In that first year in Russia his handsome features thinned. The almost innocent-looking young man turned into a hard-faced, embittered commander. Now he lived on his nerves, knowing that his life could end at any moment; knowing, too, that he must never allow himself to fall into the hands of the Russians. For by now, like the rest of *Leibstandarte's* officers, he had seen what happened to SS men who had been taken prisoner.

Now he and his men lived in that rough-and-ready, isolated world of the front, with its own morals, its own beliefs, even its own jargon. Here the world was divided into 'front swine', the ones at the sharp end, and the safe comfortable life of the 'rear echelon stallions', with their 'grey mice' (female auxiliaries), who more often or not acted as 'field mattresses' (mistresses) for the high-ranking quartermasters and staff officers. Here at the front there was only the macabre and often cruel jokes they would play on each other to bring a little entertainment into their lives. As young Gerd Bremer would often maintain to his fellow officers, 'We've been out here so long that they won't let us back into the Reich without a course in re-education. We're not safe to be let loose on those unsuspecting civilians back there', and he would add in Russian, as they were all doing by now, '*ponemyu?*'*

Once, on one of those long journeys across the Russian steppes on a train bearing their tanks to a new front, they whiled away the time drinking. One officer got so drunk that he fell and knocked himself unconscious. The others seized the opportunity. The M.O., also drunk, was enlisted. The unconscious officer was stripped and bandaged up completely so that only his eyes and mouth were left uncovered. When he finally came to, with a splitting headache, he found himself surrounded by sad-faced comrades looking down at him as he lay there, occasionally shaking their heads sadly and apparently wiping away a tear. 'Am I dying?' the officer asked anxiously. 'Doctor, tell me, please!' But all the M.O. could do was shake his head. Only when Gerd Bremer could no longer contain himself and burst out laughing did the 'dying' man realize that all he was suffering from was a monumental hangover!

Once they took two British POWs who had escaped from Italy with them to Russia as mechanics. One had been a London cab-driver; the other, named Cellars, was a former policeman from South Africa. Both of these British '*Hiwis*', as they were called (German for 'voluntary helpers'), were employed as mechanics until one day Dietrich paid a surprise visit to the division to find only these two busily working on a tank. Dietrich was pleased. He said they were an example to the whole division and asked to be introduced. His admiration diminished rapidly when he discovered that these two exemplary workers were British! Later they were ordered back to the Reich and asked if they wanted to join a unit of traitors, made up of Americans, Englishmen, New Zealanders, Canadians, etc, being formed to fight against the Russians. They declined, saying

* Understood?

they had already been there. Russia had plenty of dirt, lice, and sudden death – *but no girls*! No, thank you! As a result they survived. So, perhaps, today there is an ageing cabbie cruising around London somewhere who could boast, if he wished, that he once fought with Germany's premier SS Division, *die Leibstandarte Adolf Hitler*!

Peiper was not immune from this rough-and-ready horseplay either. It seemed to him the only way to let off steam in the harsh world of the front. Once, in a lull in the fighting, he decided to learn to fly. After one lesson with the pilot of the divisional spotting plane he decided to go solo and invited the battalion M.O. to go with him. The doctor was frightened out of his wits.

'*But you can't fly!*' he protested. 'And why do you need me to go with you?'

'It's simple,' Peiper answered smoothly. 'If I do make it successfully, then I've got you as a witness that I am now a qualified pilot. If I don't,' he shrugged carelessly, 'well, it'll be very handy to have a qualified doctor right at hand.'

Peiper made it, but the doctor nearly didn't.

Once, however, his sense of humour paid an unexpected dividend. During the *Leibstandarte's* sojourn in partisan-infected Northern Italy, Peiper got to know a high Party official, a pompous 'golden pheasant', as they were called because of their love of gold braid and decorations, to whom he took an instinctive dislike. The man was frightened out of his wits by the partisans, fearing that he would be murdered in his bed one night by them. Peiper encouraged this fear by sneaking out after dark and exploding a couple of hand grenades at the door of the Party official's door. After that he took to barricading himself in in his billet immediately the light faded and Peiper took his heavy-handed joke a little further. It had come to his attention that a small group of Jews had been rounded up by the Italians locally to be deported to Germany. Peiper had no particular love for Jews, but these were German and from his home town, Berlin. In his usual high-handed fashion, he demanded the Italians should release them to him; then he set them free. The grateful Jews were profuse in their thanks and their leader, a rabbi, asked if there were anything they could do for this SS officer who surprisingly enough had saved them. Peiper said there was. One of the group was a *kantor*, he understood. Nearby a high-ranking Party official was living, who apparently loved to hear good singing. Could the *kantor* lead the group in some songs, *preferably in Yiddish*? The rabbi said they would be only too pleased to oblige Peiper. Thus in the early hours of the following morning just after dawn, the 'golden pheasant', safely locked in his billet, was wakened *by a choir of Jews singing Yiddish folk songs*!

His reaction is not recorded, but later, when Peiper was branded by the whole Western world as a war criminal, the old rabbi did not forget. He wrote a testimony to Peiper's kindness in saving him and the rest who finally found safety in Israel.

FIVE

On 9 January, 1943, the *Leibstandarte* was sent to Russia once again. They had spent the last seven months in France refitting, retraining and preparing for Allied landings after the abortive Canadian attack at Dieppe. Now, as they were off to Russia, *Sturmbannführer* (Major) Peiper, commanding the Division's Third Battalion of *panzergrenadiere*, guessed, as did his fellow officers, that they, and the rest of General Hausser's new SS Panzer Corps, were going to be used in some new offensive operation.

They were sadly mistaken. With Stalingrad surrounded and about to surrender, the Russians had attacked across the steppe, shattering the 2nd Hungarian and 8th Italian Armies, sending the survivors streaming westwards in headlong retreat. A gap of 150 miles had been opened in the German front, into which three Soviet Armies were advancing rapidly, sweeping before them the shattered Italian, Hungarian, and German divisions. Their aim was obvious. They were out to cross the River Donetz and capture the important industrial city of Kharkov. So the SS Panzer Corps was not going into some dashing cavalry attack for which they had been trained, but into an old-fashioned infantry slogging match.

For the rest of January the SS Corps held the advancing Russians, but the commander of the 8th Russian Guards Army, itself an elite formation, probed and probed until he could find gaps. In the first week of February he found one to the north-east of the *Leibstandarte's* positions. There, the badly hit 320th German Infantry Division had held out at the small town of Stary Oskol for too long. Now its commander, General Postel, ordered his Division to withdraw and fight its way back to the Donetz. But the Division was burdened with 1,500 wounded in the midst of a terrible Russian winter and the

Russian Guards easily slipped in between the 320th and the left flank of the *Leibstandarte* at Belgorod.

Something had to be done, and done quickly. Dietrich summoned Peiper. His orders were simple. He was to take a column of ambulances, bring out the wounded and save what was left of the 320th in a fighting retreat. Although he only commanded one battalion of armoured infantry and the enemy was present in divisional strength, he set off immediately and without question.

Twenty-four hours later Peiper had his first glimpse of the 320th Infantry Division on the far bank of the River Donetz. First to make his appearance was General Postel, accompanied by a group of officers. He demanded to know why Peiper had not crossed the river to meet him with his half-tracks. Peiper, who was not impressed at all by the General who had left his men in such a terrible situation, kept his peace and replied mildly that the ice was too thin for his heavy vehicles. Postel was about to argue when an orderly officer came running through the snow to report that one of the 320th heavy self-propelled guns had just broken through the ice. Postel sniffed and stalked away, leaving Peiper and his men squatting on the decks of their half-tracks, feeling 'not too happy about things'.

Then the rest of the division began to appear. 'We all thought the same at the first sight of them. *It was Beresina!** Napoleon's retreat must have looked like this. In front those who could walk. Then the lightly wounded and finally those who had been badly hit. A miserable procession in *panje* carts (drawn by small ponies) and sledges. As these were overcrowded, some of the poor wretches had been tied to them by ropes and were dragged behind – *on their bellies*!

All night long Peiper's doctor operated, together with colleagues from the rest of the *Leibstandarte*, trying to get the most severely wounded ready for the long march still in front of them. At dawn they were off again, the badly wounded men at least now travelling by vehicle. Peiper's battalion spread out to give flank cover while the endless column began to cross the snow-bound steppe towards the bridge which crossed the stream at Udy, a long wooden structure which Peiper had taken the previous day. The hours passed leadenly under the dull threatening sky while Peiper's half-tracks ground on and on in low gear, each commander searching the horizon for any sign of the Russians. But there were none. They seemed to have abandoned their attempts to wipe out Postel's survivors. Peiper's hopes began to rise. They were going to get away with it.

But it wasn't to be. Late that day they arrived at the Udy and found

* The retreat from Moscow in 1812.

that the wooden bridge now 'consisted of smoking supports only. A Russian snow-shoe battalion had taken over the place, massacred and mutilated many of the wounded and the medics and were now engaged with the 320th in a fierce fire fight.'

Peiper's men went into action immediately. They stormed the hamlet, firing from the hip as they ran through the snow. House-to-house fighting developed. No quarter was given or expected. The SS had seen what had happened to the wounded and the Russian Guards knew there would be no mercy for them either if they surrendered. For several hours the battle swayed back and forth until virtually the whole battalion of snow-shoe troops were wiped out.

Peiper gave the order for the bridge to be repaired at once. Time was running out and night was approaching. He waited until the last of the trapped division crossed before turning – he could not risk his vehicles on the flimsy structure – to make his way across elsewhere. Another commander might have told himself that he had done enough, plunging deep behind Soviet lines and rescuing a whole division. He would have been justified in destroying his vehicles and crossing the river on foot. Instead he turned, plunged into the Russian positions once more, and succeeded in driving many miles through the enemy lines until he reached a place where he could cross without losing a single vehicle.

General Postel was not impressed. As Peiper wrote many years later: 'According to General Postel's account, there were no real fights during the retreat. He marched behind the advancing Russians without really being molested.' Peiper's role in saving his division was not mentioned in his subsequent report to higher authority.

But if General Postel was not impressed, General Dietrich was. He forwarded a recommendation to the High Command that Peiper should be awarded the Knight's Cross of the Iron Cross for his bravery and dash during this operation. In due course, in March, 1943, he received the award. Now the young battalion commander possessed not only the 'scrambled eggs', as the SS veterans called the 'German Cross in Gold', but he had 'cured his throat ache' too.* Obviously Peiper was a young officer to be watched.

All that winter and into the spring and early summer the *Leibstandarte* fought back and forth in the heart of Russia. The key city of Kharkov was taken, lost, retaken, and lost again. Finally the ruined city was retaken and held, for a little while at least. The Red Square was hastily named *der Leibstandarteplatz*; a hotly fought over bridge was

* Because the Knight's Cross was worn on a ribbon around the throat.

honoured as '*Peiperbrücke*'. But the cost had been high. General Hausser's SS Panzer Corps had lost 365 officers, 11,154 NCOs and men.

The attack pushed on. Peiper was cut off in his HQ and trapped. Reports flooded back to the main line that he had been wounded and needed to be evacuated. Tigers were sent forward to rescue him, but they weren't needed. Unwounded, but badly shaken, having suffered severe losses, he had fought his way out of the trap on his own.

The *Leibstandarte* was then thrown into the greatest tank battle in history, the Battle of the Kursk Salient, involving 900,000 men and 2,700 tanks and assault guns on the German side, and a staggering 1,337,000 men and 3,306 tanks and assault tanks on the Russian. Seeking desperately for some way out of the impasse in Russia, Hitler thought this would be the decisive blow. But even he was unsettled by the thought of what was to come. As he told General Guderian, his tank expert, before the battle, 'Whenever I think of this attack, my stomach turns over'. He should have followed his famed intuition. For the Russians were waiting for the Germans. Their spies in Switzerland, probably aided in a covert way (unknown to them) by the British SIS, had already informed them of what was to come.

In July, 1943, the titans clashed. It was a terrible slaughter on both sides under the burning sun that blazed from dawn to dusk. A solid steel battering ram of German tanks slammed into the Russian positions. The SS Corps advanced with its old élan, Hitler's words at the beginning of the battle ringing in their ears: '*The victory of Kursk must be a signal to the world!*' Kilometre by kilometre, suffering severe losses, they pushed the Russians back. But the Russians were not going to break and run as they had done in 1941 and 1942. On the morning of 12 July, 1943, under the eyes of its commander, General Rotmistrov, standing on a hilltop like some nineteenth century general, he prepared to throw in his whole Guards Army, 850 tanks and self-propelled guns, to stop General Hausser's SS Corps.

The Tigers of the *Leibstandarte*, the most powerful tank in the world, pushed forward at a steady ten kilometres an hour. On the horizon flares were dropping like fallen angels. Apart from the rumble of tracks, the steppe was enveloped in an ominous silence. On and on the monsters rumbled, hundred upon hundred of them. As the official Soviet History of the Second World War described the scene: 'The battlefield seemed too small for the hundreds of armoured machines. Groups of tanks moved over the steppe, taking cover behind isolated groves and orchards.'

Suddenly a green flare rose into the morning sky. It was the Russian signal. The silence was broken at last. Hundreds of T-34s moved forward. Scarlet flames stabbed the air. White blobs started to fly towards the Tigers – armour-piercing shot.

At top speed the much faster T-34s crashed into the sixty-ton monsters. In an instant a furious mêlée developed, both sides taking heavy losses, tanks shuddering to a sudden stop, burning furiously, their crews writhing in the charred grass as the flames rose higher, or, stranded and at the mercy of the enemy, their tracks flopped behind them like severed limbs.

As the Official History described the scene: 'The Tigers, deprived in close combat of the advantages which their powerful gun and thick armour conferred, were successfully shot by the T-34s at close range. The immense number of tanks was mixed up all over the battlefield and there was neither time nor space to disengage and reform the ranks. Shells fired at short range penetrated both the front and side armour of the tanks. . . . There were frequent explosions as ammunition blew up while tank turrets, blown off by the explosions, were thrown dozens of yards away from the twisted machines.'

Peiper's *panzergrenadiere* did sterling work in their attempts to protect the embattled monsters from the enemy attacks, rushing here and there, trying to rescue shot-up tank crews from the Russian infantry. But it was hopeless. As the day progressed the glare from the sun cutting the eye like a blade from a sharp knife, the Russians threw in more and more tanks. Desperately the SS Corps tried to push on. The *Luftwaffe* was called up. The Stuka tank-busters of the celebrated Colonel Rudel fell out of the sky like black metal hawks. The Soviet flak took up the challenge. The sky was peppered a grey-brown with exploding shells. Rudel's pilots seemed to bear a charmed life. Sirens howling, their faces pressed flat by the G-Force, they hurtled through the barrage. At the very last moment they jerked back their sticks, most of them blacking out momentarily as they did so, a myriad of lethal eggs falling from their bellies. T-34s lurched to sudden stops or went up in flames. But still the SS Corps couldn't break through, and in the end General Hoth of the Fourth Tank Army, to which the SS Corps belonged, appeared on the battlefield himself and called the attack off. Hausser had lost three hundred tanks and could not continue the drive until he received the support of the 6th Panzer Division.

Behind the now quiet front Hausser's recovery crews started dragging home the wrecks, hosing out the bloody messes of their crews with jets of water, and began a frantic patching-up job so that Hausser would have more 'runners' on the morrow. Meanwhile the staff worked feverishly, preparing plans for the continuation of the battle.

The survivors – 474 men of the *Leibstandarte* had been killed that day and twice that number wounded – swallowed a hasty meal and fell into an exhausted sleep. They'd need all their strength for what was to come on the morrow.

But, unknown to them, it was all over. There would be no continuation of the Battle of the Kursk Salient. Three days earlier the Allies had landed in Sicily. Gloomily, Hitler told his staff: 'Thanks to the miserable leadership of the Italians, it is as good as certain that Sicily will be lost. Maybe Eisenhower will land tomorrow on the Italian mainland or in the Balkans. When that happens our entire European southern flank will be directly threatened. . . . I need divisions for Italy and the Balkans. Since they can't be taken from any other place, they will be released from the Kursk Front. Therefore I am forced to stop "Citadel".'*

On 26 July, 1943, the Divisional History of the *Leibstandarte* records: 'Loading of the division on the lightning-arrow transport for an unknown destination'. They were leaving Russia once again.

---

* German code name for the operation.

SIX

Italy! The weary SS men could hardly believe their eyes as the troop trains, laden with their vehicles, began to chug up the Brenner Pass from Austria into Italy. After seven months of constant fighting in Russia, they looked forward to a long rest in a friendly country. But they were mistaken. There would be no *chianti* and *ragazzi* for the combat-weary survivors of the *Leibstandarte*.

The 'Pact of Steel', as the alliance between Italy and Germany had been called, was falling apart. Mussolini had disappeared, kidnapped by his own people. The Army was undecided. Should it lay down its arms, now that the new government had agreed terms with the Anglo-Americans, or should it attempt to defend Italian territory, both against the Anglo-Americans and the former ally, Germany? Everywhere in the industrial north the underground communist party, which had been waiting for this opportunity for twenty-one years, was beginning to make itself felt. Already armed bands of communists were sniping at German installations.

Now it was to be the job of the *Leibstandarte* to strengthen Germany's hold on Northern Italy, disarm the Fourth Italian Army which was located there, and ensure that any communist rising was crushed in the bud. Hurriedly the *Leibstandarte* was broken up into individual units to carry out this large-scale assignment, Peiper's battalion being allotted an area in Piedmont around the town of Cuneo, capital of the province of the same name.

For a while things remained peaceful. The Italian troops, on the whole, allowed themselves to be disarmed without trouble. Then on 18 September, 1943, a handsome, elegantly uniformed first lieutenant appeared at Peiper's Headquarters. He introduced himself as the official emissary of the Fourth Italian Army and demanded that Peiper should withdraw his battalion from the Province of Cuneo within twenty-four hours, or it would be wiped out to the last man.

Peiper's reaction to this bold demand is not recorded, but we do know that immediately thereafter he had a leaflet printed to be dropped on the Italian soldiers demanding that they surrender. He also warned the local burgomasters of the dangers of allowing themselves and their citizens to become involved in any hostilities between the Italian Fourth Army and the Germans. He himself drove to the burgomaster's office in the little town of Boves, which was in the centre of the Fourth Army's area, to warn the burgomaster of the consequences of helping the Army in any way.

But it was already too late. That afternoon two excited Italian policemen reported that two NCOs of Captain Dinse's company had been attacked and kidnapped in Boves. He ordered Dinse to drive to Boves immediately and free the NCOs.

Time passed and then the radio in Peiper's HQ burst into life. It was Dinse. His troop had been ambushed by superior forces. He was trapped. If help didn't arrive soon, his troop would be wiped out.

Peiper took charge himself. At the head of a column of half-tracks packed with *panzergrenadiere* and supported by self-propelled guns, he raced to the scene of action. As his column approached Boves, firing broke out immediately, from the white-painted little houses and from the surrounding hills. A machine gun burst into fire only metres away from Peiper's own half-track. Bullets ripped the length of the interior. Peiper's main radioman reeled back dead. The man sitting next to him was wounded and a slug went through Peiper's jacket and shattered his radio.

Peiper knew that his *grenadiere* wouldn't have a chance in Boves itself, with both Italian soldiers and civilians firing at them from above, directly into the open half-tracks. So he ordered the retreat. Now, as he explained many years later, 'in order to get through the place quickly, I ordered the "crickets" (name given to the self-propelled guns) to open fire'.

The heavy 155mm cannon began to blast the front houses of the village away. One by one they went up in flames, masonry showering down into the cobbled street below. Smoke started to mushroom upwards. Watching the scene through his glasses, impatient to be off once more, Peiper could see tiny figures 'in uniform and civilian clothes', as he recalled later, 'retreating under cover of the smoke into a part of the town protected from our view by a gap in the cliffs'.

Now, with the Italians retreating, Dinse's men could free themselves from the ambush. They came running towards the half-tracks and were taken aboard as the strong wind spread the blaze to more and more houses, so that it was spreading to the gap in the cliffs where the last of the resistance was probably to be found. Peiper ordered his half-tracks forward once more; but the enemy had fled. All he found was 'six cannon in a firing position and Italian soldiers and civilians fleeing over the mountains'.

The next day Peiper reported the incident to the local Prefect, General Salvi, who, according to Peiper, 'expressed the Italian government's deepest regret at the incident in Boves', which he blamed 'solely on the communists'.

That day numerous buildings were destroyed in Boves and thirty-three of its inhabitants were killed. A legitimate military operation or a criminal act? It is in the nature of guerrilla operations to render such distinctions extraordinarily difficult, if not impossible, to make. From the colonial wars at the beginning of the twentieth century up to Vietnam, the soldiers involved have always maintained that such operations were legitimate military acts. Others, mostly civilians safely ensconsed in the comfort of their armchairs, have declared the opposite.

Thus, although those who took part in the ambush at Boves were awarded a military decoration by the Italian government for their bravery, indicating that the government must have regarded the incident as a *military* operation, Peiper becomes associated, for the first time, with a 'war crime'. Events were beginning to catch up with the hero. This would be his last good year.

SEVEN

That winter the *Leibstandarte* was back in Russia for the fourth time. But this was no longer the *Leibstandarte* of 1941. The strapping young men, filled with fanatical devotion to the National Socialist cause, had vanished. Now the *Leibstandarte*'s men were no longer all eager volunteers; they were conscripts, and often unwilling conscripts at that.

By late 1943 Germany's premier SS division was accepting entries into its hallowed ranks from a dozen European countries, including even the 'decadent' enemy of three years before, France. From all over Europe they came, believing the lies of the recruiting posters in their boring provincial towns. For them the silver SS rune meant high adventure and glory, fighting for a 'united Europe against the sub-human Soviet'. In the training units back in the Reich, the 'Germanic' and 'Greater Germany' concepts were played down. Now that Germany was fighting with its back to the wall in Russia, the 'European Concept' became the motto of the day. Brunswick and Bad Toelz trained future SS officers from countries as far apart as Norway and Lithuania. Dutch SS officers taught German cadets. An American SS officer recruited Britons and Canadians into the grandly sounding, 'Legion of St George'. A Belgian, Leo Degrelle, won the Knight's Cross and became the commander of a whole Belgian SS regiment. In due course the SS division which would defend Hitler to the last in his bunker in Berlin would not be his own bodyguard – *die Leibstandarte, but the French SS Division Charlemagne*.*

These eager 'volunteers' brought with them a different ethos to that of the older SS men. They had swallowed the preposterous anti-Soviet propaganda of their instructors without question. They knew nothing

* The last Knight's Cross of the Iron Cross to be won in the Second World War was awarded to a French SS man of this division in Berlin.

of the realities of the Russian front. For them the Russians were mongrel sub-humans who were to be 'liquidated' – a favourite word – without a passing thought.

The reality shocked them. They were not prepared for the fact that the 'sub-humans' fought back, and fought back exceedingly well. Shock turned into fear and then into anger. The 'incidents' started to multiply.* From 1943 the *Waffen SS* seemed to become Europe's scourge – a ruthless, heartless collection of first-class soldiers, fighting for an ideal which had long lost its validity and a glory that had vanished years before. Now the *Waffen SS*, its ranks filled with these European 'volunteers', fought desperately, not to win any more but to survive!

The 'old hares', as the veterans of the original *Leibstandarte* called themselves, were getting tired too. As Bremer often told his fellow officers: 'When the final victory is achieved and the Army marches through Berlin in triumph, there will be a bunch of ragged, unshaven, bewildered wretches bringing up the rear. Someone will call out from the crowd, "Who are you?" But the men in rags will shake their heads as if they don't understand and say, "*Na ponemayu*" because we'll have been in Russia so long, we won't understand German any more!'

Once Peiper was called over the radio by the Division's chief-of-staff, Rudolf Lehmann, and asked why he was not moving out to the attack. Lehmann, who had known Peiper for years, hesitated to give him a direct order. Instead he said chidingly, 'What's the matter Jochen? Are you tired?'

Peiper snorted, 'Kiss my arse! I'm attacking. Out!' and snapped off the mike.

In spite of his weariness, the desperate situation on the Russian front and the ever-growing conviction that Germany was going to lose the war, Peiper could still make his daring raids behind Russian lines and turn defeat into success.

In December, 1943, he became commander of a battle group. Almost immediately his *Kampfgruppe* was thrown into battle against the Russian Sixteenth Army. Peiper personally led a night attack by his *grenadiere* on the village of Pekartschina. He roared into the place in a half-track, with guns blazing, his dreaded flame-throwers belching long tongues of flame. The village was destroyed and, as the after-action report put it laconically, the enemy was 'annihilated'.

---

* It is interesting to note that the Division *Das Reich*, which shot all but one of the citizens of Oradour-sur-Glane in France in 1944, had 8,000 former French citizens in its ranks, all Alsatian conscripts or volunteers.

Over the next forty-eight hours, *Kampfgruppe Peiper* plunged thirty kilometres behind the Russian lines in some of the worst weather of the winter. During this time he put the field headquarter staffs of *four* Russian divisions to flight and claimed some 2,500 Russians killed. Later it was stated that his bold drive had played a significant role in the successful efforts of the 48th Panzer Corps to disrupt the Russian Sixteenth Army's offensive. Peiper was awarded another piece of 'tin'. This time the Oak Leaves to the Knight's Cross.

But this was to be his last victory and his last piece of 'tin'. Now the *Leibstandarte* went on to the defensive. All that winter it tried gamely to stop the Russians, but there was no stopping them. Here and there there was a local tactical victory, but these small triumphs were of little duration. In the end the Russians always took their objective. The heart seeming to be going out of the German 'stubble-hoppers', as the infantrymen called themselves. They appeared unable to hold any position, however well prepared, for very long. Slowly but surely they were being pushed backwards towards the frontier between German-occupied Poland and Russia. Soon, as even the most optimistic of the SS officers knew, the red tide would be washing along the frontier of the Reich itself.

It was with undisguised relief that the men of the *Leibstandarte* heard they were pulling out that January. They were going to be sent westwards to rest and refit, and to meet the new threat posed in France. The long troop trains started to roll westwards once more, bearing their cargo of happy, relieved men, each one of them receiving 'the Führer's parcel',* as he crossed the Polish frontier, to give to his loved ones when he went on leave. Behind them they left Russia, savage, brutal endless Russia, where so many of their comrades now remained forever, buried in remote places whose very name they had never learned before they had died. They would never see it again.

---

* A parcel containing sausages and tea, etc, with which they could impress the folks back home. Obviously soldiers who could give away such delicacies had everything.

EIGHT

On 1 August, 1944, Adolf Hitler, still shaky from the bomb attempt on his life eleven days earlier, learned that a new Allied Army had appeared in France. But if the Army was new, its commander wasn't. The disgraced 'Blood and Guts' Patton was now in charge of the US Third Army. Hitler learned, too, that Patton had succeeded in capturing the French town of Pontaubault the day before and had established a bridgehead over the River Selune at Avranches. The gate to the whole of German-held Brittany was wide open! Already Patton had begun to push division after division across the bridge there and along a single road which led to the Breton road-net.

'Just look at that crazy cowboy general,' Hitler exclaimed to his chief-of-staff, General Jodl, whose head was still bandaged from the bomb explosion, 'driving down to the south and into Brittany along a single road and over a single bridge with an entire army! He doesn't care about the risk and acts as if he owned the world! It doesn't seem possible.'

Shaken as he was, Hitler knew he must stop Patton. Otherwise he would turn the flank of the whole German Army in France. The fate of the whole *Wehrmacht* seemed to depend upon the possession of a mere sixteen miles of territory now in American hands. Surely Patton, the boldest commander in the Allied ranks, had overreached himself this time?

Jodl seemed to think so too. There were still seven good panzer divisions on the French front, four of them SS, including the *Leibstandarte*, being held back for just such a decisive stroke as Jodl and Hitler now began to discuss. Surely they could break through to the coast, through that narrow strip of territory in American hands, and cut off Patton's Third Army in Brittany? It might be the counterattack Hitler had dreamed about ever since the Allies had landed in France in June, the great turning point which would send the enemy running for their boats.

On 2 August, Jodl sent his deputy, General Warlimont, to discuss the plan with General von Kluge, the commander of all troops in the West. The new plan, code-named 'Operation Liège', envisaged the armoured divisions being massed between Vire and Mortain. One group would kick off the attack at Mortain to be followed by the second group attacking towards Vire.

Von Kluge, called behind his back in a pun on his name 'Clever Hans' (*klug* is the German for 'clever'), asked only one question: 'When?'

Warlimont didn't know. All he knew was that the Führer would not allow any attack until 'every gun, every tank and every plane has been rounded up'.

Von Kluge didn't like that. Time was of the essence if Patton was going to be stopped. Soon Patton would be swinging right round behind him, heading straight for Paris. He wanted to attack at once. He called Jodl on the 'phone. 'We've got to strike at once. The enemy is getting stronger every day. He's already got an entire army through the Avranches gap.'

Jodl pacified him. 'Don't worry about the Americans who have broken through. The more there are through, the more will be cut off.'

Perhaps 'Clever Hans' should have persisted. But he didn't. He was a weak man. He had accepted 100,000 marks from Hitler once as a personal gift. He said he would wait. It was a fatal decision for the German Army in France. Two weeks later von Kluge was obliged to commit suicide.

One day after the conversation with Jodl, the British SIS knew of the coming offensive. For years now they had been able to read all the various German codes used by the German High Command and transmitted by the Enigma coding machine. Group Captain Winterbotham, the SIS representative stationed at General Bradley's HQ, also knew from the decodes that there was a difference of opinion between von Kluge and Hitler about the timing of the attack. But as he said later, 'I put my money on Hitler.'

He was soon to be proved right. The counterattack came too late. By dawn on 7 August the armoured divisions were to be ready to attack. Immediately Winterbotham passed on the news to Bradley, the Commander of the US Twelfth Army Group, who at once started making his preparations to meet the attack.

General Hausser, who was to command the thrust also thought it was too late. But the old soldier tried to bolster up the morale of his young soldiers and had an order read out to his men. In it he stated: 'On the success of the operation the Führer has ordered depends the decision in the war in the West. Commanders of all ranks must be absolutely clear as to the enormous significance of this fact. I expect all corps and divisional commanders to take good care that all officers are aware of the unique significance of the whole situation. Only one thing counts, unceasing effort and determined will to victory. For Führer, Folk and Fatherland!'

Shortly before dawn that day the four panzer divisions of the 47th Panzer Corps, including the *Leibstandarte* under General Wisch, struck the American line. The first action between Peiper and the *Amis* had commenced.

In spite of Winterbotham's warning and Bradley's preparations, the *Leibstandarte* was at first successful. They penetrated the link between the two US Corps, the 7th and 8th, always a difficult part of the line to defend because, although the infantrymen of each corps might only be a fox-hole's distance apart from each other, their respective corps headquarters can be miles apart. The attack started to gather momentum. Any stubborn American resistance was sealed off and left behind. By dawn hundreds of tanks had already covered four of the twelve miles which separated them from the coast and victory.

Then bad luck struck the *Leibstandarte*. They were attacked by a fighter-bomber. All along Peiper's column the flak opened up. A wall of steel raced up to meet the attacker, and the gunners were successful. Suddenly the dive-bomber staggered as if it had struck an invisible wall. Bits of gleaming metal shredded from it as it came howling down on the ride of death. With a great hollow boom, it smashed right into the tank at the point. The whole column came to an abrupt stop. The narrow road was effectively blocked by the wreckage of the plane and the wrecked tank. Peiper fumed, but there was nothing he could do about it. He had not had the foresight to put his combat engineers at the front of the column for an eventuality such as this. It was an oversight that would lead to his downfall six months later. He ordered the whole column to reverse down the road – it was too narrow for them to turn – and try and find another road leading west to the sea.

In the end they found one and again started to roll towards the coast. Looming up out of the morning mist which covered the battleground, the Tigers put the fear of God into the cowering infantry. They fled or were crushed to death in their waterlogged foxholes. The Tigers rolled on. Now they could catch glimpses of the key road leading west through gaps in the mist which was sweeping in from the sea beyond. A Sherman loomed up directly to the column's front, and another. The Tigers took up the challenge. Guns thundered. The Shermans came to a halt. Others went into hulldown positions and began firing back. The real battle had begun. Peiper had bumped into the 3rd US Armoured Division, commanded by Maurice Rose, the son of an East European rabbi who had risen from private to general inspite of the prejudice against Jews in the Regular Army. Peiper was not going to break through to the coast if Maurice Rose had his way.

Now the mist began to clear and the Allied air forces rose to do battle. The *Leibstandarte* went to ground, as the Lightnings and Mustangs came zooming in at tree-top level, cannon pounding. General von Luettwitz, commanding the 2nd Panzer Division during the attack, recalls how 'The planes came down in hundreds, firing their rockets at the concentrated tanks and vehicles. We could do nothing against them and we could make no further progress.'

Now it was the SS who were at the receiving end of the tank-busting tactics pioneered by Colonel Rudel in the Battle of the Kursk Salient the previous year. By late afternoon the attack had bogged down virtually everywhere, the fields full of wrecked and burning Tigers and Panthers.

Peiper's tank was hit. His radioman recalled years later how 'There was a great white flame. A tremendous hissing sound. Suddenly I couldn't see anything. All I could hear was the screams of my trapped comrades. I thought at first it was the result of the shell exploding that I couldn't see. Someone – perhaps it was Colonel Peiper – dragged me out of the wrecked tank and placed me on the grass. I still couldn't see. Then I fainted.' The young radio operator had been permanently blinded, but he would never lose his admiration and affection for the man who had led him into battle for the first time that day.

The next day the Germans tried again. Now they were only six miles from the sea and in parts they had virtually overrun the US 30th Infantry Division which, one day, would play an important role in Peiper's final defeat. But it was no use. The feared American *jabos* were everywhere, mercilessly shooting up anything that moved. Bradley now threw in his armour and two further infantry divisions. Everywhere the German attack was stalled and by the evening of 9 August the German War Diary noted: 'The attack of the Panzer Group in the direction of Avranches has failed to produce the hoped-for success.'

Every senior German commander knew it was only a matter of time before the counterattack would have to be called off. Hitler didn't. He blamed von Kluge. The offensive was failing because von Kluge wanted it 'not to succeed'. Angrily he summoned the Field-Marshal to his headquarters to report.

Von Kluge knew that his days and those of the whole of the *Wehrmacht* were numbered if Hitler didn't order a general retreat in France *now*. The British in the north and the Americans in the south would cut the army off. It would be another Stalingrad.

On the 15th, Dietrich, now a corps commander, told von Kluge bluntly that any general, even an SS one, attempting to tell Hitler the truth ran the risk of 'being shot'. On the following day von Kluge set off for Hitler's HQ. Just outside Verdun, where he had fought as a young man, he poisoned himself. In his final note to Hitler, he wrote, 'When you receive these lines, I shall be no more. . . . I am dispatching myself where thousands of my comrades have already gone. . . . The German people have borne such untold suffering that it is time to put an end to this frightfulness.'

But it was already too late. The German Army in France was already virtually trapped in the pocket between Falaise and Argentan. The slaughter of the Falaise Gap could begin.

After the war Wing-Commander 'Johnnie' Johnson of the RAF described the terrible slaughter of the German Army in France: 'When the Spitfires arrived over the small triangle of Normandy, bounded by Falaise, Trun and Chambois, the Typhoons were already hard at work. One of their favourite tactics against long streams of enemy vehicles was to seal off the front and rear of the column by accurately dropping a few bombs. This technique imprisoned the desperate enemy on a narrow stretch of dusty lane, and since the transports were sometimes jammed together four abreast, it made the subsequent rocket and cannon attacks a comparatively easy business against stationary targets. Some of the armoured cars and tanks attempted to escape their fate by making detours across the fields and wooded country, but these were soon spotted by the Typhoon pilots and were accorded the same treatment as their comrades on the highways and lanes.

'Immediately the Typhoons withdrew from the killing ground, the Spitfires raced in to the attack. The tactics of the day were low-level strafing attacks with cannon shells and machine guns against soft-skinned targets including all types of trucks, staff cars and lightly armoured vehicles. Here and there among the shambles on the ground were a few of the deadly Tiger tanks and although the cannon shells would have little effect against their tough armoured plate, a few rounds were blasted against them for good measure. As soon as the Spitfires had fired all their ammunition, they flew back at high speed to their airfields where the ground crews worked flat out in the hot sunshine to re-arm and re-fuel the aircraft in the shortest possible time.'

Thus the impersonal slaughter of an army of over 200,000 men went on hour after hour, all around the clock. Down below all was panic-stricken chaos as the Germans tried in vain to find some way out of the trap. One of the survivors, Karlludwig Opitz, described the slaughter ground years later: 'Vehicles pile up. Cars, heavily laden with officers' gear, honk a way through the jam, twisting past lorries in their effort to make better time. Guns are abandoned and blown up. Heavy tractors stop for lack of fuel; a couple of grenades in the engine and that's that. The huge Mercedes diesels of the workshops company are hit by rockets. . . . The fighters are having a field day. They hedgehop above the road, the engines screeching. Empty ammunition belts fall from them, rockets, grenades, machine-gun bullets, bombs, everything is thrown at the stream of vehicles.'

By now the commander of the trapped Seventh Army, SS General Hausser, had been badly wounded, but before he was put out of action he worked out a desperate break-out plan. The remnants of his five panzer divisions, led by the *Leibstandarte*, would attempt to break through the British line at Chambois. In vain they tried to form up. As the armour moved off at dawn on the 20th, they came under heavy shellfire. The tanks stalled. The shellfire grew in intensity. The officers began to lose control of their men. Gradually all order was lost in the blazing holocaust of exploding vehicles and ammunition trucks. Even the *Leibstandarte* broke, the men fleeing in terror.

By midnight it was left to individual commanders to try to make a breakout with little groups of survivors near the village of St Lambert, where the Seventh had managed to take a little road leading out of the pocket. But the single escape route was under direct fire from Canadian guns directed by a little force of Canadians under the command of a Major Currie (who won the V.C. for his actions that day), who resisted all attempts by the Germans to dislodge them from their positions.

Throughout the day Major Currie directed the Canadian guns on the German columns crossing the River Dives. Their fire caused terrible carnage. The Canadians couldn't stop what was left of the armour getting through, but many columns of horse-drawn transport were caught in the bombardment as they approached the only bridge leading to freedom. The horses stampeded. Careering through hedges and fences, the terrified animals plunged down the steep river bank, dragging their wagons and guns after them. Soon the ravine was choked with wreckage and the bodies of men and animals.

By the end of the day when the tiny gap was finally closed for good fifty thousand men remained behind in captivity and ten thousand were dead. But, of the many thousands who escaped, the brass were prominent. All five corps commanders made it, as did the Army Commander, the wounded General Hausser. Of the fifteen divisional commanders, only three didn't escape. It was the same with the regimental colonels. Most of them got through, including Colonel Jochen Peiper.

A whole army had been sacrificed on the altar of blind obedience to the Führer's command. Now these men, who knew better than anyone in Germany just how carelessly Hitler wasted lives, were safe. They would manage to return to Germany, where more young men would be waiting to refill the depleted ranks of those famed divisions with their grand-sounding names – 'The Bodyguard', the 'Death's Head's', 'the Empire'.* What would they do? Was this not the moment of truth, the time to make a stand, to tell the Führer that Germany had lost the war? Any further sacrifice of the young lives entrusted to these 'old hares', who had been fighting now for five years, would be unforgivable. Germany should make peace.

* *Leibstandarte, Totenkopf, Das Reich.*

NINE

In the first week of November, 1944, General Dietrich, the commander of the newly created Sixth SS Panzer Army, appeared at the Führer's HQ brandishing a folder marked '*Geheimkommandosache*' (top secret).

'Do you know what this is?' he bellowed when he was admitted to the presence of Colonel-General Jodl. 'I came to find out whether it's all a joke.'

Jodl, who knew that the ex-Party bully boy had just been let into the secret of the coming attack on the Americans in the Ardennes, assured him that it was not a joke. It was, indeed, a very serious thing. 'It's a plan designed by the Führer in person,' he replied.

'Then I'll protest to the Führer himself,' Dietrich exclaimed, his face flushed with anger. 'He must have based it on highly inaccurate information. Do you know what this plan means to me and my army? It means reaching the Meuse within two days, crossing it, capturing Brussels and then Antwerp. *That's all!* As if my armour would be just cutting through butter! And this pretty programme is to be carried out in the dead of winter, when the chances are nine out of ten we'll be up to our waists in snow. *Do you call that serious?*'

Colonel-General Jodl, who secretly despised this ex-NCO who couldn't even read a map properly, assured him the plan for the great surprise attack had been well thought out.

Dietrich, his face crimson now, bellowed, 'Nobody can teach me anything about an offensive! There are only thirty men left of my original division. Now I've set up a whole new armoured army. I'm a general, *not an undertaker*! I tell you that no one can carry out those orders. I insist on seeing the Führer and telling him so myself!'

But Hitler had other things to do and did not want to see the irate commander of the Sixth SS Panzer Army. Work on the great plan continued.

Dietrich, one of the original 'old fighters', who had joined the Nazi Party back in the twenties, when he had founded the little group of bully boys who protected Hitler during his speeches, out of which the SS had developed, had long realized that Germany could not win the war. Back in early 1944 he had made it clear to Rommel that if the plot to rid the Reich of Hitler succeeded and he, Rommel, would withdraw the Army in France back to Germany in order to negotiate a peace with the Western Allies, the Army would have the support of the *Waffen SS*. The man who had served Hitler so loyally for so long knew that a continuation of the war was criminal; it would mean only more of his 'boys', as he always called his SS men, would die purposelessly.

But what of those 'boys'? What of Jochen Peiper, one of those thirty survivors of the original *Leibstandarte*, which Dietrich had formed back in the early thirties? We know that he too thought little of the offensive. He thought its objectives were unrealistic and was contemptuous of the role and route assigned to his own command. Naturally, as a soldier, he would carry out his assignment whether he liked it or not. And he would remain loyal to the Führer to whom he had sworn an oath of allegiance to the very last and would regret that he did not die with him in Berlin. Unlike Dietrich he would *never* have been party to any attempt to rid Germany of Hitler.

But did he still believe in a final victory? Was he still prepared to sacrifice the lives of several thousand young men, soon to be assigned to his personal command, for a cause which had already been lost? What motivated Jochen Peiper in the winter of 1944, with the enemy pressing in on the frontiers of the Reich in the west and east, and with every major German city lying in ruins after two years of intensive bombing? He was no longer a naive, blind fanatic, if he had ever been one. He was a mature, battle-experienced senior officer, with a family of three small children to support – a man, therefore, who should have been looking forward to the future, even if it was only for the sake of his wife and children.

But that December such considerations played no role in Peiper's life. His world was breaking down all about him. Later he was to write from the death cell, 'If one does not take oneself too seriously, things here are little different from the outside. Nothing that happens to oneself is unbearable. I have seen too much of life not to be able to laugh at it; for the thinking man, it is a comedy . . . *cogito*.'

But in 1944 he could not laugh at what was happening. It was not a comedy. He had never known another world but this brutal, vulgar world of the '1,000 Year Reich'. Now it was breaking down before his very eyes, and he could not visualize any other world or any role for himself in what was to come.

Russia had left its scars on Peiper, both physically and psychologically. He had seen more than his share of death, and in his heart he knew now that violent death would be his own fate. It had to be; there was no other conceivable alternative. (That that violent death would come thirty years later was, of course, beyond his comprehension.) That knowledge and the experiences he had undergone in the artificial life of the front had cut him off from all the desires and emotions of a normal family man. His emotions were the harsh black-and-white ones of the combat soldier. Extremes were the norm.

His real family had become the *Leibstandarte*, the company of his old comrades, *die alten Hasen* ('the old hares') who had survived time and again, plus those innocent-faced eighteen-year-old lads who filled the gaps over and over again, eager for glory and an early death.

By this fifth year of war Peiper probably wanted to die. His personality had hardened into that particularly German combination of naive, almost boyish idealism, linked to the savage spirit of a brutal soldier of fortune, who knows only one loyalty. Not to God, not to his country, not even his family, but to his own unit, *die Leibstandarte Adolf Hitler*! Now, if the *Leibstandarte* was to go under, he was prepared to go under with it. There was no other alternative.

Early that December he and his men were called out to help the civil defence authorities at the nearby Rhenish town of Dueren. It had just suffered a devastating daylight raid by the US Eighth Air Force, based in Britain. Peiper was appalled by what he saw that day in the shattered town, which he didn't regard as a military target. There were dead men, women and children everywhere. 'We had to scrape them off the walls – it was that bad!' he recalled many years later. In all his combat career he had never seen so much carnage and destruction.

Now, as his unit moved ever closer to the border, his heart was filled with hatred. As he said later, 'I could have castrated the swine who did that to those innocent people of Dueran – *with a blunt piece of glass*! And those 'swine' were the Americans. So, as the day of the last great counter-offensive in the west came ever closer, the commander who would lead the Sixth SS Army's drive for the sea was filled with a burning desire for revenge.

PART II

The Crime

'Mitgegangen, mitgefangen, mitgehangen'*
Old German Saying

---

* Literally: 'Went with, caught with, hanged with'.

ONE

The regimental colonels assembled at divisional headquarters just before eleven o'clock that Thursday morning. Outside the forester's house in the remote Eifel village which served as General Mohnke's headquarters, the December fog curled in and out of the wooded hills. Everywhere the Division's vehicles were being hidden among the snow-capped firs before the morning fog lifted and revealed their positions to the *Ami* reconnaissance planes from the other side of the border, which was only ten miles away.

All was controlled, ordered haste and the waiting colonels, a little puzzled as most of them were by the sudden summons to Mohnke's headquarters, were pleased with what they saw. The Division, the losses of the summer's fighting made up by hundreds of teenage recruits and older men drafted from the *Luftwaffe*, seemed as efficient as ever.

The colonels, Skorzeny, Hansen, Sandig, etc, were similiar types – tall, heavy-set men, their chests ablaze with decorations, their uniforms immaculate, riding boots highly polished, caps neatly squared and set at the regulation angle.

There was, however, one exception – the commander of the 1st SS Panzer Regiment, who had arrived late due to the traffic clogging the narrow Eifel roads. The youngest of the regimental colonels – he was at least five years younger than most of the others – was dressed in a black leather jacket and white polo-necked sweater, his sole decoration the Knight's Cross of the Iron Cross at his throat, and his cap, with its tarnished badge, was anything but regulation, its wiring long gone, and set at a jaunty, rakish angle in the manner of the young frontline officers of the Old War. As always *Obersturmbannführer* Jochen Peiper had to be different.

Mohnke and his chief-of-staff, Dietrich Ziemssen, filled Peiper in on what he had missed, while Otto Skorzeny, the massive, scarfaced Viennese commando, who had rescued Mussolini from his mountain-top prison the previous year, watched his young comrade. Many years later he recalled Peiper as being 'tense in that cynical way of his, knowing that something big was going to happen – just *how* big I already knew from the Führer himself but he had sworn me to secrecy – but trying not to show just how eager he was to find out why he had been called to this conference almost before the sudden move to the Eifel had been completed. . . . He was like a highly-trained, nervous hound begging to be let off the leash.'

Now Mohnke got down to business. The Division had been given the high honour of leading the Sixth SS Panzer Army's attack on the American positions on the other side of the border in the Belgian Ardennes. Once again the German Army was going over to the attack, and this time they would break through to the Channel. It would be 1940 all over again.

The announcement did not come as a total surprise to Peiper. Although the Sixth SS Panzer Army had taken extraordinary measures to conceal the purpose of its move into a new assembly area, his suspicions had already been aroused by a question put to him by General Kraemer five days before. Kraemer, chief-of-staff of the Sixth, had asked Peiper what he thought of an offensive through the notoriously bad terrain of the Eifel in winter, and how long he thought it would take for an armoured regiment to travel fifty miles under winter conditions. Peiper had thereupon taken out one of his own Panthers and had driven it fifty miles over the narrow, winding roads at night. The next morning he had reported to Kraemer that the local roads 'are only broad enough for a bicycle!' Now Peiper knew why Kraemer had posed that question.

Swiftly Mohnke explained the plan of attack. It envisaged three German armies attacking westwards along an eighty-mile front driving for the River Meuse. Once the Meuse had been reached, the Sixth Panzer Army would make for the line of the Albert Canal in Belgium between Antwerp and Maastricht to meet up with General Student's Army attacking south-west from Holland. While this was going on, the Sixth Panzer's running-mate, the Fifth Panzer Army, would move parallel with the Sixth, by-passing Brussels and cutting off Antwerp, the Allies' major supply port, from the south by reaching the coast.

The aim was to severely damage the British and American armies and thus perhaps to put Britain (which was rapidly running out of reserves) out of the war, for a while at least. In the meantime Germany could deal with Russia once and for all. Thereafter Hitler could probably negotiate a peace with the Western Allies and gain better terms for Germany than at present, with the Allies actually fighting on Germany's frontiers.

None of the officers present that cold December day knew that Germany's greatest soldier (after whom the great surprise offensive would be named), Field-Marshal von Rundstedt had already passed judgement on the grandiose plan. When he heard the final objective, he had exclaimed in scorn, 'Antwerp! If we reach the Meuse, we should go down on our knees and thank God; let alone trying to reach Antwerp!'

And all of the colonels present, battle-tried veterans that they were, felt instinctively that this final objective was completely unrealistic and that the great surprise attack was doomed to failure right from the start. As Peiper stated long afterwards, 'The Battle of the Bulge would be no advertisement for either side'.

General Mohnke must have read the looks in their eyes. Immediately he paraphrased Colonel-General Jodl's words to the assembled officers: 'It is, I agree, an operation of the most extreme daring. . . . Anyway, gentlemen, there can be no argument; it's the Führer's orders.' And that was that.

Then Mohnke started to detail the routes to be taken by the various formations of the *Leibstandarte* through the Belgian Ardennes to reach the River Meuse. Peiper was to be given 'Route D'. It started at the German border village of Losheim, ran up the Ardennes heights to Honsfeld, then moved on to the River Amblève, and up to Engelsdorf (Ligneuville). From Ligneuville Peiper was to follow a very steep, winding track across country through the forest to Wanne. The River Salm would be crossed at the village of Trois Ponts where Peiper would reach a first-class road, the Belgian *Route Nationale* N-23. He would continue along this road until he reached the River Meuse, the major natural barrier in the path of the Sixth SS Panzer Army, at the town of Huy. Here he would capture the great bridge spanning the river between the cliff-like banks on both sides. As General Kraemer implored him a day later, 'Jochen, get me that bridge at Huy, even with only one tank, and you have done more than enough!'

The colonel stared at the map and showed just how unimpressed he was with Route D. The roads assigned to him had only one advantage: there was a relative paucity of bridges. Otherwise they were too narrow, too steep and too winding for his battle-group to advance with any speed – and speed was of the essence if he were to take advantage of the initial shock of the surprise attack. He told Mohnke what he had told Kraemer the previous Sunday. The roads were intended 'not for tanks, but for bicycles'.

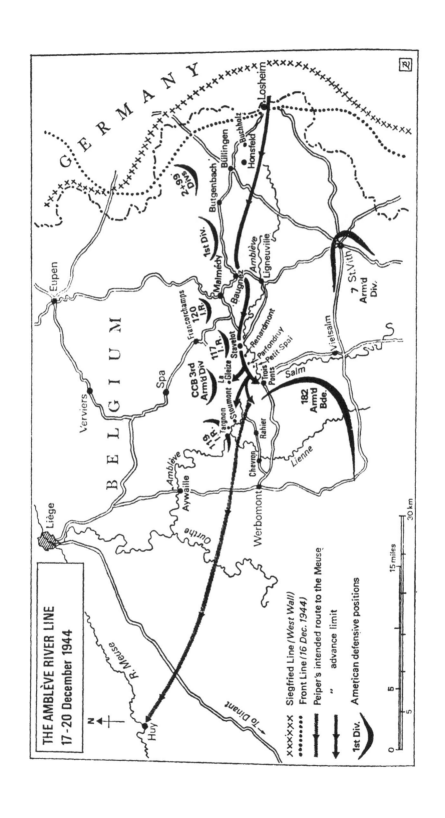

THE AMBLÈVE RIVER LINE
17-20 December 1944

GERMANY

BELGIUM

Liège
Eupen
Verviers
Spa
Huy
R. Meuse
Ourthe
To Dinant

Losheim
Buchholz
Büllingen
Honsfeld
Butgenbach
2+99 Divs
1st Div.
Malmédy
Amblève
Ligneuville
Francorchamps
120 I.R.
Baugnez
117 I.R.
Stavelot
Renardmont
Parfondruy
Petit-Spai
Trois Ponts
Salm
CCB 3rd Armd Div.
La Gleize
Vielsalm
7 St.Vith Armd Div.
119 I.R.
Targnon
Stoumont
Rahier
182 Armd Bde.
Amblève
Aywaille
Chevron
Lienne
Werbomont

N

xxxxxx   Siegfried Line (West Wall)
••••••   Front Line (16 Dec. 1944)
          Peiper's intended route to the Meuse
    "   advance limit
          American defensive positions
1st Div.

0   5   15 miles
0   5   30 km

By now Mohnke knew all about Peiper's arrogance and impatience. He simply ignored the comment and told Peiper he was to lead the drive. He hoped that Peiper would be flattered and he was.

Mohnke then went on to explain that Peiper's 1st SS Panzer Regiment was going to be enlarged and reinforced to the strength of a full battle-group. In addition to his own four companies of tanks, he was to have under command *Sturmbannführer* Diefenthal's Third Battalion of *panzergrenadiere*, two companies of combat engineers, an anti-aircraft company, a company of paras and a few Royal Tigers of the celebrated 501st Heavy Tank Company. This powerful fighting force of some 5,000 men was to be called after its commander – *Kampfgruppe* Peiper. Under his command there would also be a detachment from Skorzeny's SS Commando – English-speaking Germans dressed in American uniforms and equipped with jeeps. It would be their job to drive ahead of *Kampfgruppe* Peiper and spread alarm and panic among the *Amis* in the Ardennes.

The thought of a completely self-contained and independent command pleased the young Colonel. But there was a fly in the ointment. The force lacked sufficient fuel to enable it to reach the bridge over the Meuse at Huy. However, Mohnke consoled Peiper with the information gleaned from Intelligence that there was large American fuel supply depot at the Belgian village of Büllingen only a dozen kilometres from the border. Peiper objected that Büllingen was on Route C, allotted to the *Leibstandarte*'s running mate, the 12th SS Panzer Division (the 'Hitler Youth'). Mohnke quoted the orders of General Priess, the SS Corps Commander: 'The Corps and, under the Corps' command, the divisions have freedom of movement within this area. Thus march routes do not have to be rigidly adhered to. Each division has express permission to deviate from prescribed march routes whenever the situation demands.'

This seemed to satisfy Peiper and the discussion passed on to the infantry formations which would open up the advance for the SS armour. In Peiper's case it would be the footsloggers of the 12th *Volksgrenadierdivision*, commanded by Colonel Gerhard Engel. Engel was a former adjutant of the Führer who Peiper knew slightly from his visits to Hitler's HQ. Like Peiper, Engel had won the Knight's Cross in Russia and was an experienced soldier whose division had had considerable experience of the Eifel front during the fight for Aachen the previous autumn. Peiper, a man of few words unless he was angry, told Mohnke he would supervise the start of his own attack, scheduled to be carried in a column that would stretch for at least ten miles, from Engel's command post.

Now the conference was all but over and Mohnke concluded it by reading almost all the speech Hitler had given his generals at the initial briefing two days before, ending with the words: 'The battle will decide whether Germany is to live or to die. Your soldiers must fight hard and ruthlessly. There must be no pity. The battle must be fought with brutality and all resistance must be broken in a wave of terror. The enemy must be beaten, now or never. Thus will live our Germany! *Forward to and over the Meuse!*'

To Skorzeny, used to Hitler's flowery and impassioned oratory, the words seemed the 'usual rhetoric, intended more for inspiring the rank-and-file, who were mostly young impressionable recruits, than battle-hardened, somewhat cynical commanders. I think, "old hares", as we were, we only half-listened to Mohnke, who had steadily grown red in the face with the effort.'

Neither Skorzeny nor the others took much notice of the Führer's speech. Their minds were already racing, working out their new roles and commitments. Yet that command, 'all resistance must be broken in a wave of terror' would hang over the whole offensive like the sword of Damocles. In the years to come it would be quoted to those who survived the battle time and again until they were heartily sick of it. But those fateful words would invariably shape each and every one of their individual fates in the bitter years of defeat.

Thus the colonels departed into the foggy December day to begin their preparations for the great counterattack, unaware that they were already tainted men.

TWO

To his front the horizon flickered a dull pink. Nearby the guns thundered as vehicle after vehicle ground by in low gear, packed nose-to-tail, up to their axles in liquid mud. Here and there a mud-splattered despatch rider, carrying urgent orders, fought his way through the jam. Otherwise the weary infantry, strung out in files on both sides of the road that led to Losheim and the border, were the only ones making any kind of progress that grey December afternoon.

Peiper was furious. All day he had been waiting at Engel's HQ for the order to move out. Now it was nearly two o'clock and he had just been informed that Engel's horse-drawn artillery had clogged the approaches to the destroyed bridge at Losheim and that the combat engineers could not get close enough because of the jam to repair it.

'*Es war zum Kotzen*,'* he declared years later in the soldier's jargon he was still fond of using. 'Time was running out fast. Soon all surprise would be gone and I was still sitting on my arse in Engel's HQ.'

Now Peiper made his decision. He would do it alone. He ordered his *Kampfgruppe* to advance. Anything attempting to stop it, friend or foe, would be swept ruthlessly aside.

His men needed no urging. Like thoroughbreds champing at the bit, they were eager to be off. The lead tanks began to push into Engel's columns, forcing their way down the clogged border road, past the pitiful procession of walking wounded making their way to the rear. They were getting closer to the scene of the fighting. Above the line of firs on the hills, scarlet flame stabbed the darkening sky. Here and there there was the high-pitched hiss of the German MG 42 machine gun, answered by the slow, ponderous thump-thump of the American

* Literally: 'It was sick making.'

BARs. And all the while that dreadful background music to war, the permanent barrage, thundered.

They swung around Losheim where Peiper received a radio message from HQ telling him to detour north-west towards the Belgian hill village of Lanzerath. Leaving the road, he set off across the fields. But suddenly the column came to an abrupt stop. Peiper sprang out of his Volkswagen jeep and ran forward. A panther was slewed across the track next to a smoking brown hole. Its right track was gone and the driver was propped up on the deck, face pale, holding his bleeding head. 'Mines, sir!' the commander reported crisply, as ahead there was another muffled explosion. In the sudden burst of violent flame, Peiper caught a swift glimpse of a half-track lurching to a halt.

He nodded grimly. The damned paras who had attacked through this area early that morning had failed to lift the mines. Now *Kampfgruppe* Peiper was going to have to pay the butcher's bill. '*Los*,' he barked. '*Vorwarts!*'

He sprinted back to his own vehicle. He was going to clear the mines by rolling his armoured vehicles over them; there was no other way.

It was midnight, 16 December, 1944. It had cost Peiper three tanks and five half-tracks to get this far, but now his *Kampfgruppe* was approaching the village of Lanzerath, recently captured by the men of the 3rd Parachute Division's Ninth Regiment and it looked 'as if it (the Ninth) had gone to bed instead of waging war'.

As his own vehicle clattered into the one and only street, he could see no sentries, no guides, nothing.

'They've got their CP over here, sir,' one of his men called up from the darkness.

Peiper dropped stiffly to the ground and strode over to the place's single café, Cafe Palm, which was the Ninth's HQ.

Peiper was disgusted with what he saw inside. The Ninth, commanded by a Colonel Hoffmann, a recent rakeout from Goering's Air Ministry in Berlin, had stopped the war for the night, as if this was a peacetime exercise. Unshaven paras were asleep everywhere. A soldier snored on top of the zinc-covered bar. In the corner a bunch of white-faced prisoners, some of them wounded, from the US 99th Infantry Division waited glumly for the morrow. One of them, Dr Lyle Bouck, then a twenty-one-year-old lieutenant, wrote to Peiper many years later describing that midnight scene. 'About twelve, a group of officers came into the room. They were busy and excited about the situation. A map kept falling off the table near the far side of the room. One of the officers stuck the map against the wall with two bayonets.

A few of the officers left the room and then returned, mad about something. One of the German soldiers was wounded badly in the arm. He was in shock and shouted, *"Panzerfaust, panzerfaust, panzerfaust!"* One of the officers made this soldier go upstairs with the other wounded. He seemed to feel this wounded soldier might grab a weapon and kill the wounded Americans'.

For the first time, even before Peiper's command had really been engaged in combat, we have a reference to prisoners being murdered in cold blood. But at that moment Peiper, the man who had stuck the map to the wall with the two bayonets, had other things on his mind than killing prisoners. His anger was directed at the para commander, who seemed not to have the vaguest idea of what was going on.

At once the two colonels were engaged in a terrible row. Peiper treated the older and more senior officer more as if he were a private than a regimental commander. What was the situation on his front, he demanded. Were there *Amis* in the woods beyond Lanzerath? Why had the Ninth stopped? Why weren't they moving forward?

The Colonel was full of excuses and apologies. The 3rd Parachute Division had suffered severe losses in Normandy and he, Hoffman, had been posted to it after years on the Berlin General Staff; he knew little of frontline conditions. According to him there were enemy soldiers everywhere in the woods to his front. There were minefields and fortified positions up there too. Someone had reported the noise of *Ami* tanks moving about in the darkness.

Peiper had no patience with the middle-aged para. Point-blank he demanded to know whether Hoffmann had personally reconnoitred the *Ami* positions in the woods. Hoffman was forced to admit that he hadn't.

Peiper knew from experience how young soldiers sent on patrol to find out about enemy positions would agree among themselves that they were heavily defended without ever going near them; it was safer that way. Accordingly, without asking Hoffmann's position, he 'phoned the major commanding the para battalion dug in outside Lanzerath. How did he know about the Americans supposedly facing him, Peiper asked.

The Major admitted he had received his information about the *Amis* from one of his company commanders. Peiper insisted that the company commander, a captain, be brought to the 'phone. Somewhat embarrassed the captain stated that he, too, had not seen the American defences personally. He had received the details from an NCO.

Peiper slammed down the phone in rage. He turned on Hoffmann. He didn't ask; *he demanded.* He wanted Hoffmann's 1st Battalion for a dawn attack through the woods. He wasn't going to risk his precious *panzergrenadiere*. Let the paras suffer if there were indeed *Amis* out there.

Hoffmann blustered, but in the end he gave in, pointing out that although his regiment had been only one day in combat, he was now being forced to give up one third of his effectives. Peiper was not interested. He rapped out his orders to the para major commanding the 1st Battalion, who already realized that his men were going to be used as cannonfodder by Peiper. They would attack their first objective, Buchholz railway station, at zero four hundred hours; till then he and his officers could get what sleep they could. For his part, Peiper refused to turn in, just as he would for the rest of the offensive. There were more important things than sleep.

Now it was 17 December, 1944. As he sat there at the scrubbed wooden table. Peiper little realized that this would be the most momentous day of his life, one which would determine the rest of the thirty years still allotted to him. When all these men, German and American, snoring around him had long slipped back into the comfortable obscurity of civilian life, the events of this Sunday would ensure his notoriety until the day he was murdered.

THREE

Peiper stood in the turret of his Panther. Behind him the long column prepared to move off once more. Just as he had suspected, there had been no sign of the enemy in the woods outside Lanzerath. The inexperienced paras had simply been scared of their own shadows.

Peiper was not scared as they began to move through the trees. Four times he had had his tank 'shot away from under him', as they said it in the *Leibstandarte*. In Normandy earlier that year, his tank had taken a direct hit from an American shell and his radioman, standing right next to him, had been hit and blinded. Once a Russian had fired a full magazine of machine-pistol slugs at him from only twenty metres away – and missed! Always his luck had seemed to hold; in five years of active war service he had not suffered a single scratch, although the *Leibstandarte* had been virtually decimated four times over.

Five minutes later the point of *Kampfgruppe Peiper* caught up with a long column of US vehicles, moving through the pre-dawn darkness, bumper to bumper in low gear, towards the west and safety – artillery pieces, jeeps, ammunition trucks, half-tracks, anything with wheels, filled with tired and frightened men. These survivors of the previous day's battle now formed part of what they were already calling 'the big bug-out'. The American Army in this part of the Ardennes was in full retreat and Peiper was going to make full use of the resultant panic and confusion.

Already he needed fuel desperately. Later he told his US interrogators that his command had used as much fuel in those first twenty-five kilometres of the advance, due to the rugged, hilly terrain, as would have normally take him fifty kilometres. He decided, in view of the confusion all around, that he would take a chance and rush the *Ami* petrol dump at Büllingen. But first he would have to pass through the little hamlet of Honsfeld, held, he knew, by men of the US 99th Division. With a bit of luck, if he kept close to the retreating Americans, he might be able to slip through without a fight. He decided to chance it.

Just as dawn started to break, the SS stole into Honsfeld. No one seemed to notice them. Like grey timber wolves the paras guarding the flanks crept from house to house.

At the entrance to the village a Lieutenant Robert Reppa of a cavalry reconnaissance squadron was sitting on a very hard chair trying to get some sleep when he noticed a change in the sound of the retreating traffic. There was no denying it. This was the sound of tanks! He sat up, suddenly wide awake. Swiftly he strode to the door and flung it open. Before him was a huge tank, twice the size of any Sherman. He shut the door swiftly and gasped, 'My God, they're Germans!'

In the street the paras were rounding up the Americans who had been forced to surrender. One of them, Corporal Fruehbeisser, recalled later, 'There were *Amis* everywhere. We disarmed them at once and broke up their weapons. Then we drove them onto the street and started to count our loot – in chocolate and cigarettes.'

'Just as we were about to mount up again all hell broke loose. Firing started from windows at the far end of the village. An American mortar opened up on us too. Our tank commander turned his cannon round on an enemy machine-gun nest and scored a direct hit.'

Fierce house-to-house fighting began in the village street. Tracer zipped back and forth. Ricochets howled off the stone walls. Men screamed with pain. From all sides came the pitiful cries of the wounded, pleading for help.

'Suddenly *Ami* dive-bombers came falling out of the sky,' Fruehbeisser remembers. 'Almost immediately our mobile flak took up the challenge, as they came screaming down. The air was full of flying 20mm shells. The *Amis* broke and roared away. But almost immediately thereafter, *Ami* shells began falling on Honsfeld. All was confusion and sudden death.'

Peiper made a snap decision. He was not going to allow himself to be bogged down in the unimportant hamlet. He ordered a few tanks to stay behind and help the hard-pressed paras. A hasty reconnaissance was made up the road to the next village of Heppenbach. The report was negative. The road was a sea of mud, no good for heavy tanks. Peiper decided he'd try another. Judging by the fire to his right that their running-mate, the 'Hitler Youth', was having a hard time of it and not making good progress, he ordered a change of direction. They were to head for the 'Hitler Youth's' Route C and drive for Büllingen and the fuel dump. *Kampfgruppe* Peiper rattled away into the grey gloom, leaving Honsfeld behind it – and the first recorded crime committed by the SS.

Peter Mueller, a middle-aged farmer, German-born and German-speaking (he had become a Belgian after the Treaty of Versailles) had left the border village of Manderfeld the previous day. Leaving his family behind at Holzheim, he had fled with his fifteen-year old nephew who the previous autumn had refused to dig positions for the Germans and now feared he might be arrested by the returning Gestapo. Together they aimed to reach the safety of 'Old Belgium', that is the pre-1920 part of the country. But they had been overtaken by events here in Honsfeld and had been captured with the surviving Americans in the main firing line.

'I saw one of the Americans raising a white cloth in token of surrender,' Mueller stated twenty-five years later, 'while another ran into the nearby stable to shoot the animals. The Germans forced their way into the house and drove us into the street. An SS man who saw us ran across and shouted, "Man, do you want to be shot? Tell them you didn't do any shooting." I told him we were innocent and we'd only been there to look after the animals, but they didn't believe me.'

It was clear what Peiper's men thought. Throughout their long fighting retreat through France and Belgium the previous summer, they had been constantly ambushed by the French *Maquis* and the Belgian *Armée blanche*. Indeed the commander of the 'Hitler Youth', General Kurt Meyer, known as 'Panzermeyer', had been captured by Belgian guerrillas. Now here were German-speaking civilians found together with American soldiers who had been firing on them just minutes before. Obviously these civilians had been helping the *Amis*. *They were partisans.*

'We were formed into a column,' Mueller recalled later, 'and marched to Lanzerath. All the way I thought of trying to make a break for it. But there were too many German soldiers coming from the opposite direction. Finally we stopped outside the Café Palm. An SS man said to me and my nephew, "All right into the barn. You're going to be shot at once!"

'My nephew, Johann Brodel, cried, "But we're Belgian!"

'In that same moment he fell to the ground, hit by a bullet in the back of the head. I turned round to see what had happened and heard a second shot which struck me in the neck. A third shot then hit me behind the ear. I swayed, turned round several times and fell to the ground, though I didn't lose consciousness. I feigned death and then, when the soldier had disappeared, I sat up.

'My nephew was dead. Covered with blood, I ran across to the house of Christoph Schuer opposite the barn. Although the house was full of soldiers, they started to bandage me up. When Christoph Schuer heard what had happened, he shouted at the soldiers, "Are you crazy, shooting harmless people?"

'He had said too much. The SS soldiers present were only restrained by two Army officers who were there. Finally they said we would have to wait until the *Sturmführer* arrived and made his decision. So I sat there and waited. Finally the *Sturmführer* arrived and, looking down at me, he said: "Mueller, you can go. The matter has been dealt with."

'Sadly I began to trail back home without my nephew.'

So here we have our first recorded 'atrocity', the shooting of Johann Brodel. Yet, examining it more closely, we are immediately plunged into that confusing triangle of Germans, Americans and Belgian civilians of German tongue and origin, which was going to plague investigators after the battle for years to come. Was Peter Mueller, born a German, yet obviously regarded as loyal by the Americans (they had evacuated all 'unreliable elements' from the border villages the previous autumn) as innocent as he sounded? Why did he abandon his wife and children to flee westwards with his nephew? Would the advancing Germans really be interested, in the middle of a life-and-death battle, in one fifteen-year-old youth who the previous September had refused to dig ditches for them? Was it just chance that the two of them were captured in the midst of fighting American soldiers?

We know, too, that the infantry fighting in Honsfeld were paras. But Mueller talks of SS. The scars prove that Mueller was shot, but by whom? An SS man or a para? And why was he shot? Was it just an outburst of personal rage? Or was it on orders from above? Or did the killer think that the two Belgians were partisans, belonging to some Belgian resistance movement (there were several active in the Ardennes area)? Many questions with few satisfactory answers. Yet that morning the tone had been set and *Kampfgruppe* Peiper had already been stamped with the mark of Cain.

FOUR

Perhaps the first of the remaining thirty-six Belgian civilians in Büllingen to spot the SS that Sunday morning was Albert Kohnenmergen. With the rest of the civilian population still there, he had been allowed by the Americans to remain behind in order to look after the cattle and, like the good farmer he was, he was now risking the shells beginning to fall on Büllingen to check his cows. But he didn't get far. 'I saw a tank stop down below the village. It bore the American star on its side, but standing in the turret there was a German soldier. Next to it there was a group of American soldiers who were just as surprised as I was.'

Some of the defenders of the village did not surrender straight away, however, as Peiper's men swiftly overran the place, destroying twelve American liaison planes on the ground and capturing 50,000 gallons of fuel. As Kohnenmergen recalled later: 'Fourteen Americans hid in the house belonging to Mathias Bormann. A Tiger tank went over a mine just outside the house and lost a track. The soldiers were discovered, and the German NCO who was ordered up to repair the damaged track, shouted to us, "All you civilians should be shot!"'

But there was no shooting of civilians in Büllingen that day. The only civilians killed were those hit by American shellfire, though, as we shall see, Peiper's men would be accused of slaughtering Belgians in Büllingen too.

Nor were any Americans killed. Peiper needed all the prisoners he could lay his hands on in order to help re-fuel his tanks. At any minute he expected the arrival of the point of the 'Hitler Youth' and he didn't want to add to an already confused situation by having his vehicles mixed up with theirs.

Shortly before nine Peiper was ready to move off again, while heavy US artillery fire from the right began to land on his stationary column, causing some casualties. Later Peiper was to tell his interrogators that he believed that some of the local civilians were spotting for the Americans, the fire was so accurate. Even if they had been, Peiper had no time to do anything about it. He had to be on his way.

Leaving a small covering force behind, he set off after nine, turning to the main Büllingen-St Vith road, which surprised the Americans dug in between Büllingen and the next large village, Butgenbach. Now he started to make progress. With his tanks full, with no opposition and on a fairly good road (for the area), he pushed ahead swiftly. Three miles beyond Büllingen, without having had a shot fired at the column, Peiper paused to interrogate a surprised American lieutenant-colonel captured riding alone in his jeep. Now he gave the point to an old comrade, Major Werner Poetschke, a highly decorated veteran of the Russian front, who, ironically enough, had been born in Brussels in 1914.

It was an unfortunate decision – for Peiper. For Major Poetschke, the only one of any authority who knew what happened next, was killed in action in Hungary three months later. Poetschke pulled away with the point, leaving Peiper to deal with the American who had some exciting news for him. At Ligneuville in the Hotel du Moulin there was the headquarters of the 49th Anti-Aircraft Brigade, commanded by a General Timberlake. Peiper had never captured an *Ami* general before and the prospect excited him. He wanted to add him to his already varied collection of Yugoslav, Greek, Italian and Russian general officers whom he had captured in the past. He started to plan how he might reach the pretty tourist village and capture the unsuspecting *Ami* general. At that moment General Timberlake was just sitting down to his Sunday lunch before the balloon went up.

FIVE

The average Anglo-American is not very original in his choice of names to substitute for foreign ones that he cannot pronounce. The history of the two world wars is full of 'Piccadilly Circuses', 'Times Squares', 'Hellfire Corners' and the like. The crossroads at the Belgian hamlet of Baugnez, a couple of farms and a shabby inn, was no exception. Because it marked the spot where five roads met the GIs called it 'Five Points'.

That morning the isolated crossroads where the roads to Malmédy, St Vith and Büllingen meet, had been exceptionally busy, for a Sunday. Long convoys of armour and truck-borne infantry had been moving through the crossroads ever since dawn. They belonged to the US 7th Armored Division, hurriedly moving south from Holland to help the hard-pressed 106th Infantry Division in the St Vith area.

Now, just about midday, the last vehicle of the Seventh Armored's Combat Command R had just cleared the crossroads and one of the two MPs directing traffic there decided it was a good time to go down to Malmédy in the valley below and eat. He left his companion, Private Homer Ford, to deal with anything else that might come through during his lunchtime.

The crossroads was deserted save for the lone MP, his carbine slung over his shoulder, his white-painted helmet tilted to an angle, stamping his feet to keep out the cold. In the farmhouses across the way the locals and the German refugees who had been billeted on them from the Rhineland, were having their meagre Sunday dinner. Behind him in the Café Bodarwé the plump owner, Madame Bodarwé, was chatting with her neighbour, farmer Henri Le Joly. The only sign that there was a war on was the steady thump-thump of the heavy guns to the east. At about that time Madame Solheid, who lived at the edge of the village of Thirimont on the heights above the crossroads, was 'startled by the sound of heavy motors coming from the direction of Ondenval. Then I saw the first German tank coming down the *Voie des Allemands*, heading for our village. The Germans had arrived!'

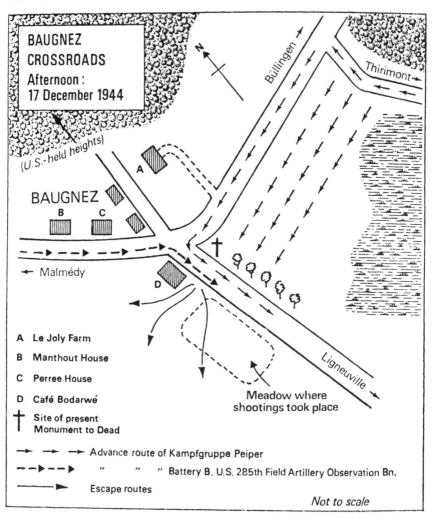

BAUGNEZ
CROSSROADS
Afternoon:
17 December 1944

(U.S.-held heights)

Büllingen

Thirimont

BAUGNEZ

A Le Joly Farm
B Manthout House
C Perree House
D Café Bodarwé
† Site of present Monument to Dead

Meadow where shootings took place

Ligneuville

Malmédy

→ → → Advance route of Kampfgruppe Peiper

‑‑►‑‑►   "   "   " Battery B. U.S. 285th Field Artillery Observation Bn.

───► Escape routes

Not to scale

The leading German tanks of Peiper's point had gone via the short cut, whose name dated back to the time when it had been used to transport leather from Malmédy to Germany. Suddenly the tanks came under a sudden and alarming salvo of American shells, twenty-eight in all. But they fell harmlessly into some fields and the tanks pushed on towards the village church. Here they divided into two groups: the first drove directly for Baugnez, the other group turned left and headed for Ligneuville.

At the same time as the German point left Thirimont, another convoy left Malmédy, the principal town of the region, and began the slow grind up towards the heights at Baugnez. It belonged to Battery B of the 285th Field Artillery Observation Battalion, which was making its way from the Hurtgen Forest area of Germany to the Belgian town of Vielsalm. Battery B was a relatively green outfit, as yet unattached to a corps or division, but in the manner of its death this day it would achieve greater fame than it would have ever have done on the battlefield. For most of the men shivering in the backs of the two-and-a-half-ton trucks had less than two hours to live.

The lead vehicle arrived at 'Five Points' around 12.45 am. Later Ford, the military policeman, testified that it was a jeep in which Second Lieutenant Virgil Lary sat. He was going to play a big role in what was to come. He asked Ford the way to Vielsalm. Ford directed him towards the road to St Vith, Route Nationale N-23, and kept the convoy moving smoothly around the corner.

According to Henri Le Joly, however, one of the leading jeeps halted and a soldier who 'looked like an officer', followed by two others, entered the Café Bodarwé. 'Vielsalm?' the officer inquired and pointed down the road. Madame Bodarwé nodded her agreement.

In French, the American asked Le Joly if he had seen the Germans. The farmer pretended not to speak French, although just before the officer had entered, he had been speaking Walloon French with Madame Bodarwé. Le Joly was basically German. He had been born German, his father had been a German soldier in the First World War, and although he spoke French like a native, he preferred the local German dialect.

'For me Germany was the country of my birth and my homeland,' he recalled years later. So he shook his head as if he didn't understand. The officer shrugged and left.

Private Ford, satisfied that the convoy was safely through, turned and started to walk to the café to warm up. He had only gone a few steps when he heard the crump of a shell exploding nearby. Startled, he swung round. To his horror, from the secondary road which led to Thirimont, he saw German tanks heading for the crossroads at full speed! Others were bumping across the wet field beyond the trees, firing as they came, heading straight for the road to St Vith.

In the café a frightened Madame Bodarwé cried, 'Shall we go into the cellar?'

Le Joly shook his head. Outside more and more guns were joining in. High explosive shells seemed to be exploding everywhere.

'No,' he yelled above the thunder of the guns, 'the barn, if anywhere! If the house starts to burn, we'll never get out of the cellar.' But they had no time to run to the barn. On both sides of the road the ditches were filled with stalled and shattered trucks. For a moment Ford remained glued there, watching the artillerymen scrambling for cover, as German infantry began to run across the field towards the ambushed convoy. Suddenly he realized his own danger. He shouted to a handful of the artillerymen running down the road towards him to take cover behind the Bodarwé barn; then he pelted towards it himself.

Second Lieutenant Lary's jeep was hit almost immediately. He and Captain Keele, in charge of the convoy, dropped into a ditch with their driver, Corporal Lester.

'Do you think it's a patrol which has broken through, or is it too heavy for a patrol?' he gasped to Keele.

Keele shook his head. 'No, the fire is too intense,' he replied.

'Let's crawl up this ditch,' Lary suggested, 'and try to make a stand for it beside that house we've just passed.'

Keele agreed and the three of them started to crawl towards the café.

They didn't get far. Suddenly they were startled by the rattle of tank tracks. Lary chanced looking up. Almost upon him there was a great metal monster, the black and white cross on its side all too obvious. He dropped back and pretended to be dead. The tank passed. They pressed on, but it was already too late to make a stand. In front of the café some twenty GIs stood, their hands raised in surrender.

Lary attempted to rally them but was dissuaded by a Corporal Daub. The latter pointed up the road and said, 'Look up the road.'

A whole column of German tanks and half-tracks was rolling towards them. Lary sprinted back to the ditch where Captain Keele was still crouched. 'Are you hit, Captain Keele?' he asked. There was no answer. Lary tried again.

'No,' Keele hissed. 'Go away or they will come back and kill me!' Lary persisted and finally Keele joined the rest, hands high in surrender.

Now the survivors of the artillery bombardment waited for the Germans. Lary pulled off his officer's bars, hoping that he would be taken as an enlisted man. Why, he never explained later. He must have known, green though he was, that an officer enjoyed extra privileges in a POW camp.

From his hiding place in the café, Ford watched as Major Josef

Diefenthal's *panzergrenadiere* started to round up the prisoners. Then Diefenthal (the only one to be definitely identified later because of the light-tan US combat jacket he was wearing) ordered the firing to cease. They herded them into a field beyond the café, robbing them as they did so of their warm winter gloves and whatever else they could find on them.

Madame Bodarwé and Henri Le Joly now felt it safe to come out and watch the scene. Nothing ever happened in Baugnez. This was something to be watched. A little later they were joined by a fifteen-year-old boy named Pfeiffer from one of the border villages. So now there were three civilian witnesses of what was now going to happen.

Ford, for his part, just had time to watch Diefenthal's men move off in the direction of Ligneuville when the outbuilding where he and other fugitives were hiding was surrounded by SS troops. They were ordered out into the open. After being searched and looted, Ford and the rest joined the other prisoners standing in rows of eight in the field, hands still raised.

Now, save for one lone American, Sergeant Warren Schmidt, feigning dead, his body immersed in a foot of water, there were only prisoners at the crossroads – and dead men. Curious yet uneasy, the three civilians stared at the prisoners. They seemed very much at ease and not at all despondent at the sudden change in their fortunes. Le Joly didn't share their calm acceptance of their fate. Although he was glad that his own people were back in control, he did not like the mood of the young SS men. Back in the café one of them had told him that three *Amis* had escaped from Büllingen by stabbing their guard with a penknife. To him it seemed that the excited young soldiers were in a vengeful mood. They need a strong hand to control them and there seemed to be no officer present. He decided that he'd soon sneak back to the safety of his own farm. Anything could happen.

Colonel David Pergrin, the dark-haired, bespectacled commander of the 291st Engineer Battalion, stationed at Malmédy below the crossroads at Baugnez, heard the boom of cannonfire and the snap and crackle of small-arms fire above the noise of the traffic blocking the street below his office. Immediately he guessed that Battery B, which he had seen leaving the town, had run into some kind of trouble at the crossroads.

For a while longer he concerned himself with his own very precarious position. Malmédy was full of fleeing soldiers, panic-stricken civilians, and over three hundred German nationals, evacuated from the bombed Rhineland. Now all he had to defend the place was a handful of engineers who had no combat experience. It was a damned difficult assignment.

Already the trouble had started. Civilians and soldiers packed the streets, heading west. No one would stay and fight and systematic looting had begun.

At quarter past one an artillery outfit started to fight its way through the crowded streets. Pergrin tried to convince the major in charge to stay and defend Malmédy, but he refused. Pergrin hurried to the local replacement depot, where 400 infantrymen waited to be sent up the line. He asked the officer in command for these men, but he was turned down. The replacements were being sent back to Liège. Now Pergrin knew he was on his own with his single company of engineers.

Uncertain and unhappy, he decided to make a personal reconnaissance of the crossroads to see what was going on. At half past two he set off up the hill, accompanied by Sergeant Bill Crickenberger, both of them armed with submachine guns. As their jeep ground up towards the heights brooding silence seemed to settle on the fog-shrouded Belgian countryside. Pergrin, not an imaginative man, felt that there was something seriously wrong somewhere.

Beyond the 291st's road block where the road really began to climb steeply, Pergrin left the jeep. He and Crickenberger climbed the hillside in the hope of getting a clear view of the crossroads. To the right the view was obscured by the fir woods, but to the front everything was clear. Pergrin swept the area with his glasses, but he could see neither friendly nor enemy troops.

For a few moments he and the NCO crouched there, wondering what to do next. Then the silence was broken by the rattle of small-arms fire and the screams of men either in pain or anger, or perhaps both.

Perhaps five minutes later four men came running screaming through the woods to the observers' right. Pergrin ran to help them. They were the MP, Homer Ford, and three companions. All were mud-stained, wounded and panic-stricken.

Almost incoherent with shock and fear, they babbled something to the Colonel about the Germans having killed *everybody*.

At about the same time that Pergrin and Crickenberger made contact with the men who had undergone whatever they had undergone on the hilltop, Lieutenant Tom Stack, one of Pergrin's officers, and another lieutenant were probing the road in front of the roadblock when suddenly three figures rose from the ditch in front of them.

Stack pointed his weapon, but, seeing they were American, lowered it again. He stopped the jeep and took them aboard. They too were virtually incoherent with fear. The two officers whipped the jeep about and raced back to the Battalion Aid Station in Malmédy.

Back in Malmédy, the survivors were fed and dried out. After they had calmed down, Pergrin began to question them. In essence, they all told the same story. They had surrendered to the SS, had been placed in a field near the Cafe Bodarwé, where they had been shot down by their captors in cold blood. They had been unarmed and had made no attempt at resistance. The Germans had simply begun shooting into their massed ranks without any apparent reason. As Pergrin listened, it began to dawn on him that up there at the crossroads something akin to a massacre had just taken place. It was something that ought to be reported to higher headquarters.

At 3.50 pm he wrote out a report for the US First Army, to which command his unit belonged. In it he detailed the basic facts of the 'massacre' and the approximate number of men involved. Some hours later that same message, amplified a little, would be on its way to the 12th Army Group, to which the First belonged, and from there it would go on to SHAEF for the eyes of the Supreme Commander, General Eisenhower himself. It read: 'SS troops vicinity L 8199 captured US soldier, traffic MP, with about two hundred other US soldiers. American prisoners searched. When finished Germans lined up Americans and shot them with machine pistols and machine guns. Wounded informant who escaped and more details follow later.'

The world, however, was going to learn about the 'massacre' on the hilltop, not through official channels but through the Press; for it happened that just about this time two American newspapermen arrived in Malmédy. Hal Boyle and Jack Belden of *Time* magazine, both attached to First Army in Spa, had celebrated one of their usual Saturday night 'wing-dings' the night before. As a result they had risen late to find all of their fellow newspaper correspondents had long since departed for the front. Belden and Boyle, both suffering from hangovers, had taken a leisurely breakfast and then set off to find the new surprise battle in the Ardennes. Boyle had gone through the disastrous Battle of the Kasserine Pass back in February, 1943, and thought he knew just how fast the Germans could advance.* Although First Army staff officers had assured him the Germans would make slow time through the rugged Ardennes, Boyle thought differently. He told his less experienced companion that the most likely place to see some action this Sunday would be at the crossroads at Baugnez.

* See C. Whiting, *First Blood, the Battle of Kasserine Pass* for further details.

Now his hunch was paying off. As the shocked survivors of whatever had happened at Baugnez crossroads kept coming in (in the end there were seventeen) Hal Boyle knew he had a scoop – the 'best story of the war'. He listened while three of them told what had happened, 'half-frozen, dazed and weeping with rage' (as he wrote later).

Some time later Lieutenant Lary, who had apparently been brought in by a friendly Belgian farmer, shook a bullet out of his boot and with it the bloody remains of his toes. 'We didn't have a chance; we didn't have a chance,' he kept repeating.

After Lary, the last survivor, had told his story, Boyle and Belden raced back to Spa to file their scoop, a story which would go round the world.

Yet already the story of the events on the crossroads at Baugnez was becoming confused. Colonel Pergrin in 1965 wrote, 'Upon reaching the woods, three American soldiers came limping out, screaming incoherently. One of the three was a Lieutenant, who had been wounded in the heel. If my memory serves me at this late date, this man was Second-Lieutenant Virgil Lary.'

However, when interviewed by Mrs Janice Giles five years later for her book *Those Damned Engineers*, Lary made his appearance 'around midnight' and not at 2.30 pm and was 'able to give final confirmation (of the massacre) clearly, concisely and coherently'. Now Colonel Pergrin maintains that 'Lary was in perfect control of himself, calm and collected. He related the entire sequence of events coherently and in good detail. There was no evidence of hysteria. Like a good officer, he made a good clear report.' Yet Belden and Boyle had apparently already interviewed Lary, shaking the 'bullet out of his boot' and moaning that 'we didn't have a chance' hours earlier.

Already the confusion surrounding the events at the crossroads had begun.

Already the news had started to spread. By six o'clock that evening Major-General William Kean, First Army's Chief of Staff, knew of the matter. He wrote in his diary: 'There is absolutely no question. General Vanderbilt (the TAC Air Force Commander) has told every one of his pilots about it during their briefing.'

A little later news of the 'massacre' reached the division in the line. According to the US Official History of the battle, (*The Ardennes: Battle of the Bulge*) 'there were American commanders who orally expressed the opinion that all SS troops should be killed on sight and there is some indication that in isolated cases express orders for this were given. In one fragmentary order published at that time (issued by the headquarters of the 328th Infantry) it is stated: "No SS troops or paratroopers will be taken prisoner, but will be shot on sight." '

In a way the 'massacre' came as a godsend to the American High Command. In that first week of the Battle of the Bulge there were wholesale surrenders by US troops. Indeed a mere fifteen miles away from where the survivors were now being questioned, 10,000 American infantrymen of the ill-fated US 106th Infantry Division* were now considering a surrender, which would be the biggest surrender of US troops (apart from Corregidor) since the Civil War. Now High Command could point out to the waverers that surrender was no good either; the Nazis would shoot you anyway.

President Roosevelt made the point quite clear when he was informed of the incident by the Secretary of State for War, Stimson. 'Well now,' he said, 'the average GI will hate the Germans just as much as do the Jews.'

So now the Americans were out for blood and the immediate future boded ill for the unknown SS men and their commander who had commited such a heinous crime at those remote crossroads. Already the US authorities had begun to fashion the noose for the man who commanded those 'SS killers'. It would be a vengeance that would shake the whole foundation of American military justice. It would involve no less a person than the Supreme Commander, General Eisenhower, when he later became President of the United States; it would further the career of a maverick in US politics and give rise to 'McCarthyism', and result thirty-odd years later in the brutal murder of a broken old man in a little French village.

But now, on this December Sunday, the first soft flakes of snow had begun to drift down at Baugnez, mercifully starting to hide what had happened there that day. By midnight the seventy-odd bodies sprawled in the field next to the smouldering ruin of the burned out Café Bodarwé would be covered by the snow. It would be another two months before they would be seen again (at least by American eyes) and by then the US authorities would know who the chief 'SS killer' was – *Obersturmbannführer* Jochen Peiper.

* See C. Whiting, *Death of a Division* for further details.

SIX

The small town of Stavelot, with a civilian population of 5,000, was the first place in 'Old Belgium' in Peiper's path. The heights above the old town had formed the border between Imperial Germany and Belgium prior to 1914.

Peiper, on the morning of Monday, 18 December, was concerned with crossing the River Amblève which flowed through the town. For infantry it presented no problem; they could wade it. But for tanks it was tough. The only way they could cross the Amblève was down the narrow cobbled road that came from Ligneuville, over the bridge and then up a steep rise into Stavelot. But what if the bridge were mined, or the *Amis* had anti-tank guns positioned on the rise?

Peiper was worried. Already his *panzergrenadiere* had checked out the approaches to the stone bridge. They had found no *Amis*; that eastern bank of the Amblève was free of the enemy. This was reported to Peiper, but still he hesitated to chance sending his tanks across that narrow, hump-backed bridge. As he wrote afterwards, 'My own situation was obscure. Clear was only that things did not develop according to plan. We were low on gas. Food was not worth mentioning. I sensed that my flanks were completely open and had the uneasy feeling that nobody followed either. No radio contact would be established since my departure. My current messages were never acknowledged nor did I ever receive any. . . . I now felt for the second time that the big strike was over. . . . The very fact that nobody followed and I could not reckon on any supply coming up convinced me that a further breakthrough lacked all prerequisites. When I advanced I did so more or less in order to leave the mouse trap and regain some terrain more favourable for tanks.'

So Peiper decided, reluctantly, to leave the 'mouse-trap'. He would take the bridge and move up to Stavelot market place where he would turn west to Trois Ponts. Here he would cross the River Salm and push on via Werbomont to the River Meuse.

'Drive hard,' Kraemer had urged him, 'and hold the reins loose.'

So, in spite of his misgivings, he decided to do just that. Getting into his command vehicle, he ordered Private Zwigart, his driver, to start up.

The morning stillness was shattered by the roar of tank engines and at once came the howl of mortars as Peiper began his covering barrage on Stavelot. The leading tanks, accompanied by infantry, began to rattle down the steep hill towards the bridge. In Stavelot confusion reigned. Caught by surprise, the frightened GIs manning the road block on the far side of the Amblève pulled back to the bridge itself. The mixed force of infantry and engineers holding the bridge itself was infected by the panic and started to withdraw up the hill, leaving the bridge uncovered.

The senior officer present, a Major Solis of the 825th Tank Destroyer Battalion, ordered one of his remaining cannon to be placed in position near a house where it could fire over the Amblève. Hurriedly it was emplaced and the owner of the house, a Belgian civilian, volunteered to observe for the gun crew, which he did quite accurately, setting fire to two houses along the route being taken by Peiper's men.

But the hits didn't stop Peiper. In the lead Captain Krenser's 1st Tank Company, accompanied by Diefenthal's *panzergrenadiere*, swung round the last bend in the steep descent and saw the bridge just in front of them. At that same instant a salvo of shells crashed down. Krenser went reeling back, badly wounded. For a moment the attack stalled, but Lieutenant Hennecke took over and got the men moving once more. Hennecke knew the *Amis* would have prepared the bridge for demolition, but he didn't hesitate. He ordered the leading two Panthers to rush it.

The young tank commanders, with that blind obedience which made the *Leibstandarte* the outfit it was, moved forward. The first one swung round the bend. Only yards away was an enemy anti-tank gun. The Americans fired. At that range they couldn't miss. The shell hit with a great hollow boom. Flames shot out of the Panther's turret, but it didn't stop. The momentum was too great. With a rending crash, it battered its way through the anti-tank gun, ramming two Shermans in its ride of death and finally came to rest, burning fiercely. No one got out.

But the young commander's sacrifice had not been in vain. The second Panther rattled across the bridge, followed by the *panzergrenadiere*. A confused fight broke out. The Americans began to pull back to the market place, the *grenadiere* at their heels all the time, giving them no chance to dig in.

Peiper did not wait to mop up what was left of the Americans. Somewhere behind him was the 3rd Para Division; let them do a little fighting for a change, he told himself. He ordered the point, under Hennecke, to head for Trois Ponts.

Hennecke had just about cleared Stavelot when he received the order. But at that instant a group of civilians appeared from nowhere. Later the official Belgian Government inquiry maintained that they had come 'to look at the tanks'. Hennecke's men didn't hesitate. They opened fire with their machine guns, spraying the street to left and right with lead, and then they were gone, rattling up the main road to Trois Ponts. Behind them they left fourteen-year old José Gengoux lying in a pool of blood, shot in the stomach, and his sister Germaine sitting on a kitchen stool, staring in bewilderment at her shattered arm, which would soon be amputated.

Whether Hennecke's gunners took the civilians for American soldiers, whether they thought they were partisans (after all, it was about here that the unknown Belgian had acted as a spotter for Solis' gun-crew) or whether they were just plain blood-thirsty, we shall never know. That hour of combat in Stavelot was too confused. But as far as the Royal Commission, set up in January, 1945 by the Belgian Prince Regent to investigate the events in the valley of the Amblève, was concerned, the first atrocity committed by *Kampfgruppe* Peiper against Belgian civilians had just taken place.

Trois Ponts got its name from the three bridges located there – two over the River Salm and one over the River Amblève. On that Monday morning, 18 December, 1944, it was Peiper's intention, coming down the road from Stavelot, to pass under the railway viaduct, turn sharply south along the same road, cross the Amblève, follow the valley road for a couple of hundred yards and turn west at right angles to cross the Salm and enter the main part of the village. Thereafter he would take the main motor road to Werbomont. That was his intention. But with its exceedingly narrow roads and very tight turns that were difficult for heavy tanks to negotiate, Trois Ponts was ideally situated for defence. On that morning, too, the defenders were mainly combat engineers (from the same group as those in Malmédy), with their specialised knowledge of minefields and explosives. Trois Ponts was

going to be a hard nut to crack, even for *Obersturmbannführer*
Peiper; and the Colonel had not reckoned with four young Americans
who where soon to die, named McCollum, Hollenbeck, Buchanan and
Higgins.

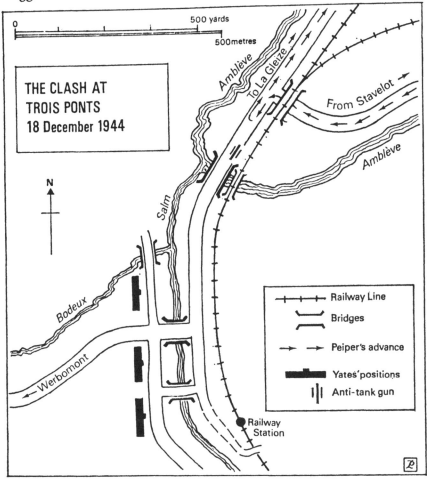

THE CLASH AT
TROIS PONTS
18 December 1944

It was just by chance that they were there at all. The four men were
an anti-tank crew from the 526th Armored Infantry Battalion. Just as
they were passing through Trois Ponts, the half-track pulling their
puny 57 mm anti-tank gun had slipped a track and they had been left
behind. Colonel Anderson, in charge of the defences, had requisi-
tioned their cannon and placed it in position where the Stavelot road
entered Trois Ponts. It was a chance happening that would influence
the whole course of the fighting in the Amblève valley.

At noon the point of *Kampfgruppe* Peiper reached Trois Ponts.

Nineteen Panthers started to crawl towards the railway underpass where the engineers were frantically laying mines. The leading gunner fired a burst. The engineers scampered for cover. Peiper's own engineers doubled forward. In a matter of minutes they had cleared the mines and the advance continued once more.

Now the tanks started to move towards the underpass. The leading Panther rumbled under the railway line, swung sharply round the bend, its engines roaring – and stopped dead. Directly in front of it was the puny little 57mm cannon – a totally ineffective weapon against the mighty Panther with its heavily armoured glacis plate. It was David versus Goliath. Confident that he could win the uneven fight, the tank commander ordered his gunner to take up the challenge.

The gunner fired. The long, heavy, overhanging cannon spat fire. But in his haste the gunner missed. The shell whizzed harmlessly past the little gun.

Now it was the turn of the Americans. The gunner pulled back the firing bar. Flame streaked from the muzzle. Its trails leapt up. There was the hollow boom of metal striking metal. The Panther reeled, as if struck by a sudden tornado. Its track flopped uselessly in front of it and it came to a sudden halt, smoking furiously.

The next Panther ground its way past its stricken mate in low gear. It opened fire at once. Its gunner had a better aim than his predecessor. The American gun disappeared in a ball of flame, throwing the shattered bodies of its crew into the air. They were dead instantly, but their sacrifice was not in vain.

Yards away a sweating crew of engineers under the command of a Captain Yates had about finished fixing their explosive charges to the Amblève bridge. Now, as the Panthers started to roll once more, Yates waited no longer. '*Blow her,*' he yelled and brought his raised right arm down smartly. The sergeant pressed the plunger. There was a muffled roar The bridge started to shake and wobble. Then, with a great rending sound, the bridge went up. Moments later the whole centre span starting tumbling in bits and pieces into the water of the river below. *The bridge across the Amblève existed no more.*

Peiper contained his anger with difficulty. After the war he told his interrogators, 'If we had captured that bridge at Trois Ponts intact and had had enough fuel, it would have been a simple matter to drive through to the River Meuse early that day'. But he controlled his anger and concentrated on his map. Now he was in another 'mouse-trap'. How was he going to get out of it? Meanwhile his *grenadiere* took up the challenge offered by Anderson's men. They swarmed forward, firing from the hip, as the engineers worked feverishly to get the second bridge across the Salm ready for demolition.

Across the river Anderson watched the Germans through his binoculars. After the war he said that he had seen them swarm into the area between the underpass and the blown bridge, where he saw 'one German soldier, without any provocation whatsoever, kill an old Belgian man and woman who, by the bundles they were carrying, were only trying to evacuate their home'. Colonel Anderson thus became the first and *only* American eye-witness of the killing of Belgian civilians by Peiper's men.

Peiper made a quick decision. There was only one escape route he could take – to the right of the underpass, leading through the steep gorges of the Amblève valley to the hilltop village of La Gleize. Here, he hoped, he would be able to find other bridges across these damned Belgian rivers which would bear the weight of his heavy tanks. With a bit of luck he might be able to cross the Amblève there and get back onto the Werbomont road.

He gave the orders to start up once more. His tanks creaked forward. Behind them McCollum, Hollenbeck, Buchanan and Higgins stared at the sky with unseeing eyes, unaware that their sacrifice meant that Peiper was entering a trap from which he would never escape. When in the end he returned down this road, it would be as a fugitive in the night, exhausted and starving, a beaten man.

SEVEN

Peiper had an easy passage to the village of La Gleize, abandoned only an hour before by other engineers of Anderson's command. He had been attacked from the air admittedly, but with no great losses. Now he rolled through the village – a circle of low white stone houses grouped round the small church and school – until he reached the most prominent building, the Château Froidecour, until recently the US headquarters, where the harassed elderly gardener was still trying frantically to remove the American star that had decorated the place during the Americans' residence. Peiper paused at the farmhouse in the Château's grounds and sent out a reconnaissance party to check his front. Their task was to find another bridge for the *Kampfgruppe* capable of bearing Peiper's heavy tanks.

Meanwhile the rest of his long column, which stretched some twenty miles, was being dive-bombed again by American planes from the 365th Fighter Squadron, guided to their tempting targets by unarmed Piper Cubs from the US 109th Tactical Reconnaissance Squadron. Observing the attacks, one of Anderson's engineers positioned on a hill overlooking the column thought it was like watching a Hollywood movie from the front seat.

Peiper's men didn't share his feelings. They were severely shaken up by the persistent attacks against which they could do little, especially the men of the 7th Tank Company, which was now beginning to crawl through Stavelot in low gear.

Here and there houses were burning. Their own infantry seemed to have vanished and the tankers knew they were easy meat for American bazooka-men in the narrow streets. So they did what they always did in towns – they used 'marching fire', just as General Patton always insisted his own men of the US Third Army should use. They took each bend with extreme caution, blazing away with their turret machine-guns indiscriminately at anything that moved. Presumably they suspected that partisans and American snipers were dug in everywhere. Just before the 7th cleared the town, one of the German tanks stopped outside *Les Quartiers*, where the Lambert family lived. Two of the SS tankers got down from the turret, pistols in hand, and hammered on the door. Monsieur Lambert himself opened it. Without a word, one of the SS men shot him. Stepping over the body, they entered the hall, crying, 'Are there Americans here?'

Madame Lambert, who had heard the shot but did not realize that her own husband was dead, came out of the kitchen, followed by her daughter Claudine, and faced the two murderers. The two young men demanded beer. Trembling with fear, she hurried to the kitchen to fetch some. It was only when she returned with two bottles of Stella Artois that she realized her husband was lying there on the threshold in a pool of his own blood.

'Laughing,' as the Report of the Official Belgian Inquiry put it, the two SS men seized the bottles and drained them in one go. Swaggering out, they did not even look down at their victim as they stepped over him. The second 'atrocity' by Peiper's men had been committed in Stavelot.

Meanwhile, further up in the hills, as the light began to fade, US engineers were finishing wiring up their explosives at the Habiemont Bridge. Corporal Chapin set up his detonator box in an old German sentry box some hundred feet from the bridge. From here he could see a short stretch of straight road before it bent right around the cliff-like hill.

By now it was 4.45 on this December evening and the light was almost gone. Suddenly Chapin spotted tanks crawling forward through the gloom. For a moment the engineer could not believe the evidence of his own eyes. In the grey gloom they had something eerie and ghost-like about them. A sudden crack, followed by a burst of fire from the leading tank, told him that there was nothing supernatural here. They were all too real!

The first shell hurtled past Chapin, alerting him to his own danger. Behind him his boss, Lieutenant Edelstein, was waving at him frantically to blow the bridge, as the German tanks crawled nearer and nearer. Chapin hesitated no longer. He turned the key and saw the streaks of blue light running along the charges. Next instant the bridge shuddered, heaved violently, and disappeared in a cloud of flame and dust. Habiemont Bridge was no more. Peiper's route to the west was blocked once more – *and this time it was for good.*

Again Peiper had no sleep. As it began to grow light that Tuesday morning at La Gleize, a weary, unshaven and worried Peiper began to give Major Knittel, commander of his reconnaissance battalion, his orders for the day. But before he had got far Knittel interrupted his chief with some urgent news of his own. 'They've killed a good few at the crossroads,' he said.

'The crossroads?' Peiper queried, looking up from his map.

'Yes, the one at the turn-off for Engeldorf,' Knittel replied, 'There are a lot of *Ami* dead there.'

Peiper did not know it then, but Knittel had given him the first news of what America was already calling 'the Malmèdy Massacre'. But at that moment he wasn't particularly interested. There were far more important matters to be dealt with that morning.

During the night units of two American divisions, the 30th Infantry and the 82nd Airborne, had infiltrated into the Amblève valley and were beginning to form a hard front which could well stop any further movement westwards. Moreover his own communications with the rest of the *Leibstandarte* and the 3rd Para Division's follow-up were being threatened by the Americans who had retaken Stavelot. He therefore ordered Knittel to take a mixed force of tanks, armoured cars and self-propelled guns back down the road from La Gleize and drive the Americans out of Stavelot.

Knittel set off on his mission immediately. At Trois Ponts he paused to divide his command. One half, under Captain Koblenz, was to advance on Stavelot along the road which ran north of the River Amblève. The other, under Captain Goltz, was to take the steep secondary road that leads through the hill villages of Ster, Parfondruy and Renardmont. There they would deal with the particularly troublesome artillery battery that was located somewhere behind the little village of Stoumont. At midday the two columns set off on their separate ways. But not for long. The American artillery observers soon spotted Koblenz's group as it rolled along the valley road, hemmed in by the Amblève on one side and the steep hillside on the other.

Almost at once heavy shellfire started to fall on the German column. It was impossible for them to find cover. Vehicle after vehicle was hit. For a few minutes more Koblenz tried to battle on, but it was hopeless and in the end he yelled to his men *'Volle Deckung!'*. They needed no urging to take cover. They abandoned their vehicles and scurried up the hillside, leaving the shattered, burning column behind them.

Now the American artillerymen turned their guns on Captain Goltz. He had succeeded in driving through the three hillside hamlets, where in most cases the Belgian civilians had run out to welcome them, thinking that the Germans were returning Americans. Shells started to fall on the column with frightening accuracy and almost immediately Goltz started taking casualties. One minute after the terrible barrage had begun, his ammunition truck blew up with a terrible roar, scattering dead and wounded on all sides. Goltz had had enough. He yelled to his men to pull back and take cover.

By late afternoon Major Knittel, who had set up his headquarters in the cellar of a burned-out farm near Trois Ponts, was beginning to receive reports that both Koblenz and Goltz were pinned down. Worse, he knew now that his battalion had suffered nearly three hundred casualties; it had lost a third of its strength in a single afternoon.

If we are to believe the Belgian investigators of the events in the Amblève valley in that third week of December, 1944, the killings started without warning or any provocation on the part of the local civilians.

In spite of the battle raging on the Stavelot – Trois Ponts road, one Belgian civilian, Tony Lambert-Bock, decided he needed a shave. All morning he had hidden in the cellar of his house with his family and neighbours and he was still unwashed and unshaven from the night before. He could tolerate it no longer. He was going upstairs to get cleaned up. His family warned him not to go to the bathroom. He ignored their warnings and went up the steps. A few minutes later the people cowering in the cellar heard a single shot. For a while no one dared to go and see what had happened. But in the end Lambert-Bock's son ventured cautiously upstairs. He found his father lying dead on the floor, shaving soap lather still wet on his face. Frantically he clattered down the steps to the cellar, crying: '*Ils ont tué mon papa!*'

An hour later five German soldiers of Knittel's command forced their way into the house occupied by Monsieur and Madame Georgin, Madame Counet and the Nicolay family. While two of the Germans checked the upper floors, the remaining three herded the civilians into the kitchen. Suddenly an SS-man cried, 'You have been hiding bandits here!'

The terrified Belgians knew what the German meant. '*Bandits!* No,' they cried. 'We've had no Americans here. Not one.' The Germans didn't believe them. For some reason one of the SS-men selected Louis Nicolay and ordered him outside. Obediently the Belgian followed the

SS-man out. After a few moments the silence was broken by a single shot. Madame Nicolay started to cry. Now Monsieur Georgin was ordered outside. He, too, followed tamely. But he was not going to let himself be slaughtered like a dumb animal.

The SS-man indicated that the Belgian should walk past him. As he did so Georgin heard the click of a safety catch being released. He hesitated no longer. Summoning up all his strength he bolted for freedom. The German fired. Georgin dropped to the *pavé*, hoping the SS-man would think he had been hit and was dead. For five endless minutes he lay there, his heart thumping. Then, judging the coast clear, he started to crawl for the river bank. Finally he made it and dropped into the icy water of the Amblève. But now his luck ran out. Just as he was clambering up the far bank, a machine gun opened up (later he said he believed it was a German weapon). Georgin felt a tremendous blow on his arm. He fell heavily, his arm nearly severed by machine-gun fire. Much later, when he was able to return to his home, he learnt from neighbours that his wife and the rest of the civilians who had sheltered in his house had been found dead. Presumably the SS had shot them. At least that is what the Belgians thought.

That evening and far into the next day, the trapped men of Knittel's command shot civilians all along the road between Stavelot and Trois Ponts. If we are to believe the Belgian Inquiry four civilians were shot at Ster and fifteen outside the village. At Renardmont nineteen were shot and, again according to the Inquiry, 'their houses set on fire to hide the crimes'. In Parfondruy twenty-six were killed. At the Hurlet farm, just outside Parfondruy, a dozen civilians were mown down by a German armed with a machine gun. When the Germans had gone, the frightened villagers crept out of their hiding places. Among the dead, whose ages ranged from nine-month-old Bruno Klein-Terf to seventy-eight-year-old Josephine Grosjean-Hourand, they discovered only one survivor – two-year-old Monique Thonon, covered in his dead mother's blood, but still alive.

From the Belgian sources, the only ones available, it would seem that the SS had only one objective – to slaughter as many civilians as possible. Yet, with only one exception, no one *saw* the SS actually kill the civilians. The one exception was Madame Regine Gregoire, who had been born Regine Heuser in the border village of Manderfeld and who spoke fluent German. (At the time of her birth she had indeed been a German citizen.) That day she had decided to take refuge with her two children in a house owned by the family Legaye.

During the evening American soldiers took over the top floors of the house and began sniping at the SS. The Americans told the Belgians sheltering in the place to keep quiet and nothing would happen to them. Around six that evening a scared GI came into the cellar and told the Belgians that the Germans were attacking in force and they were clearing out.

Shortly afterwards, the refugees were startled by the snap-and-crackle of small-arms fire outside. It ended with startling suddenness when the door was flung open and a grenade came tumbling down the steps – standard operating procedure in house-to-house fighting. It exploded harmlessly with a tremendous roar. But the next one sent steel shrapnel hissing everywhere. Madame Gregoire yelled with pain, as something struck her leg like a red-hot poker being applied to her flesh. She had been hit, but she had no time to examine the wound. From above a harsh voice commanded, '*Heraus . . . raus hier!*'

The Belgian civilians panicked. Knowing that she spoke German, they urged Madame Gregoire to tell the SS that they were only civilians. Hastily she did so, but all she got for her pains was the order, '*Raus!*' Madame Gregoire led the exodus of the civilians, telling the waiting SS that there were only women and children in the cellar, plus two old men. The SS nodded their understanding and told her to tell the rest to go into the garden. Obediently they did so and there they were ordered to sit down by the hedge.

Meanwhile the sergeant in charge ordered Madame Gregoire to look after a comrade who had been wounded in the fight for the house. Obediently she complied. She found the young soldier lying on a couch, bleeding badly. One of the SS handed her a dressing and snapped angrily, 'One of you civilians here shot at us.'

According to her own account, she replied, 'That's not true. It's you who wounded one of us with your grenade.'

'Don't shout at me like that!' he yelled and kicked her. Then he went out, leaving her to bandage the wounded soldier.

Soon thereafter the house echoed with the sound of shooting once more. A terrified Madame Gregoire saw two soldiers armed with a rifle and a revolver systematically shooting the civilians squatting by the hedge.

Later the dead were discovered to be Prosper Legaye (66), his wife Marie (63), their two daughters Jeanne (40) and Alice (39), and their granddaughter Marie-Jeanne (9); O. Lecoq (68), Henri Daisomont (52), who had sworn he would never flee his native village again as he had done in 1940, his wife and two daughters; Madame Bouxhet (41) and her four children.

According to Madame Gregoire this group was followed by

Madame Prince, who cried out just before she was shot, 'Oh, my poor children without a mother!' and her three children; plus a Madame Lecoq (60), her daughter Jeanne, Madame Remy and her son Jean.

When it was all over the only survivors were Madame Gregoire and her two small children. Angrily she told the soldier standing next to her, 'There was nobody here but innocent civilians.'

The soldier answered, according to her, 'The innocent must pay for those who are guilty. The people of Stavelot have been harbouring American soldiers.'

With that she was led away into another cellar, where she was rescued forty-eight hours later by the returning Americans. Surprisingly enough she, the only eye witness, was not shot by the SS.

In the end, according to the Prince Regent's inquiry, one hundred and thirty civilians were slaughtered by the SS in the Amblève valley. There was not a single family in the whole valley who had not lost a relative. On the basis of one soldier killing one civilian, if we are to believe the official Inquiry, *every third soldier of Knittel's command had murdered one man, woman or child*!

Next morning, when the Americans counterattacked, Corporal Eliot of Colonel Anderson's engineers saw how the massacre was used to bolster the morale of American soldiers about to attack an SS position on the other side of the River Amblève. He recalls: 'Before starting the job we were shown what had happened in the cellar of one of the houses. Apparently the Germans had gathered all the people left in the town into the cellar of one of the houses and there they proceeded to punish them for befriending the Americans. Two small children actually had their heads smashed in. Men were dismembered and shot. One pregnant woman had been cut open and left to die. This scene was viewed by hundreds of GIs.'

Later, Eliot remembers, 'The tanks drove right over the enemy positions and literally buried them alive. Prisoners were then rounded up and brought to the bridge. Here they were stripped of all American clothing and marched, some practically naked, most without shoes, to that particular cellar and forced to view the awful scene in it. From there they were marched through the town into a wooden section from whence shortly came the sounds of much shooting. I had always read Americans treated prisoners justly.... I have always been glad that the 291st (Engineer Battalion) had no part in the executions.' The reprisals had begun.

EIGHT

The big gun which had been firing at close range all that day finally ceased and Peiper, in his new headquarters in the cellar of the little schoolhouse at La Gleize, now ordered his senior American prisoner to be brought to him. The prisoner, a broad-faced, handsome American in his late twenties, was Major Hal McCown, a battalion commander of the 30th Infantry Division's 119th Regiment. He had been captured the previous day while on reconnaissance. Now he faced his captor for the first time, and wondered what the German commander, obviously trapped for good in the hilltop village with elements of three US divisions pressing in on him, wanted of him.

But Peiper didn't want military information. Instead he offered the West Pointer, who had lost his first battalion command almost as soon as he had taken it over, a cup of ersatz coffee and began to chat in good English. Thus we have our only portrait of Peiper during the battle from a non-German source. The talk rambled on half the night and McCown was struck not only by Peiper's fanaticism but also by his sense of humour and obvious culture.

'We can't lose,' Peiper told the American, while outside the battlefield settled down till dawn. 'Himmler's new reserve army has so many divisions that your G-2 will wonder where they came from.'

He went on to talk, in general, about his devotion to the German cause. 'Oh, I admit many wrongs have been committed. But we think of the great good Hitler is accomplishing. We're eliminating the communist menace, fighting *your* fight. And the Führer's concept of a unified, more productive Europe – can't you see what good that will bring? We will keep what is best in Europe and eliminate the bad.'

Warming to his theme, Peiper proceeded to describe the enthusiasm with which the German invaders had been received in other European countries. Everywhere millions of French, Belgian, Dutch, Norwegian, Finns etc had flocked to the German banner, accepting the Führer's concept of 'One Europe' united in the common cause against bolshevism.

In part Peiper was right, of course. Virtually every country in Occupied Europe had supplied a major formation up to the strength of a division to the SS to fight the Russians in the East. Poland was the only exception. Indeed at that moment, in embattled La Gleize, Peiper had Frenchmen, Belgians, Dutchmen, even Rumanians in his own *Kampfgruppe*.

But Peiper was also subscribing to the new propaganda line dreamed up by the 'poison dwarf', the undersized, club-footed Minister of Propaganda, Josef Goebbels. Now that Germany could no longer win the war, he had created the concept of a European 'crusade' against the sub-human Bolsheviks.

Yet if McCown did not understand Peiper's fanaticism, he did slowly begin to admire him. The young SS officer was only a couple of years older than himself, but obviously he had seen much more of war. For a professional soldier like McCown, who would one day become a general, that was always a cause for admiration. Besides he was obviously a man of higher intelligence and superior military experience than many of the over-aged, poorly trained colonels who led infantry regiments in the US Army, McCown couldn't help thinking. Slowly, as that December night dragged on, with the candles flickering and throwing shadows on the flaking cellar walls, McCown, like all Americans who came to know Peiper later (even those who wanted him sentenced to death), came under the young German's spell.

McCown was prompted to ask about the safety of the hundred and fifty prisoners-of-war in Peiper's hands, locked away in basements and cellars all over the village. By now he was certain that Peiper was the man whose outfit had reportedly shot a large number of unarmed American prisoners after they had surrendered near Malmédy. Would that be the fate of his hundred and fifty fellow prisoners? Many of Peiper's teenaged soldiers didn't strike him as very stable. Keeping his own counsel, he asked casually about the German treatment of prisoners on the Russian front.

Peiper smiled. 'I'd like to take you to the Eastern Front,' he said. 'Then you'd see why we've had to violate all the rules of warfare. The Russians have no idea what the Geneva Convention means. Some day, perhaps, you Americans will find out for yourselves. And you have to admit that our behaviour on the Western Front has been very correct.'

1. This photograph of Peiper was taken just before the German invasion of Russia in 1944.

2. Colonel General Sepp Dietrich, founder of the *Liebstandarte*.

3. A rare photograph of Peiper taken in 1941 when he was Himmler's adjutant. He is standing at the back on the left. In the foreground, from left, are Hess, Himmler and Bormann.

4. The Café Palm today, in which Peiper spent the first night of the Battle of the Bulge.

5. Colonel David Pergrin, who first found the survivors of the massacre at Malmédy.

6. Henri Le Joly, one of the few witnesses of the massacre to survive.

7. American troops examine the bodies of the victims of the massacre.

8. The bridge at Stavelot today. For ten hours it was the most important bridge in Western Europe. If Peiper had crossed it in time the whole course of the Battle of the Bulge might have been changed.

9. After the battle at La Gleize.

10. This camp outside Nuremberg housed 160,000 German prisoners. It was here that Peiper was found by CIC Agent Richard Lang.

11. The Trial, 1946. Defendants at Dachau.

12. The Malmédy Judges. General Dalbey and Colonel Rosenfeld are fourth and
    fifth from the left.

13. Colonel Everett (centre) and Colonel Rosenfeld are questioned by a war correspondent.

14. Colonel Ellis (left) cross-examines Lieutenant Perl (right). An interpreter sits between them.

15. Peiper on trial.

16. Dietrich in the courtroom at Dachau.

17. Peiper just before he was murdered.

18. The village of Traves in France where Peiper was murdered in 1976.

19. The last tank of the *Leibstandante* is still at La Gleize.

Feeling more confident now, McCown, who had only observed one breach of the Rules of Land Warfare during his three and a half days of captivity (the Germans made American prisoners unload ammunition), asked, 'Colonel Peiper, will you give me your personal assurance that you'll abide by the rules of Land Warfare?'

Solemnly Peiper looked at his captive. 'You have my word,' he replied.

Their conversation rambled on for hours, McCown successfully pumping his captor for information. Peiper obviously believed in the new V-weapons which the Führer kept promising the German people. But he obviously didn't believe in the long-term objectives of this great new offensive – the Channel ports. He was fighting in a nearly hopeless situation. But because he was a good soldier he would continue to do his duty.

By the time the new dawn came creeping into the village McCown thought he had the measure of the German Colonel and the whole Nazi system. If Peiper no longer had any heart for the battle and had resigned himself to defeat, then there was not much hope for the whole rotten Nazi structure. He felt, nevertheless, that Peiper would honour his promise to leave his prisoners unharmed.

The great 155mm started firing once more. The cellar shook and the candles flickered wildly. Peiper got to his feet wearily and nodded to the guard to take McCown away. Thus they parted, in a strange kind of way friends in spite of being foes, and another day of war began.

Just about the time that Peiper and McCown parted, another captive and his captor were meeting for the second time. This time the roles were reversed; the prisoner was a German, Captain Koblenz, and the captor an American, Captain Kurth, attached to McCown's own outfit, the 30th Infantry Division. Koblenz and what was left of his group had been captured two days before. At that time nine of the captured SS men had been threatened with death by the enraged GIs when the local Belgian police chief had shown them the bodies of the civilians massacred, supposedly, by the SS. Just in time their company commander, Captain John Kent of the 117th Infantry Division, had prevented the killing.

Now Captain Kurth, himself German-born and a refugee to the States, went to work on Koblenz and his men with the gloves off! Each man was cross-examined individually, the gruelling interrogations continuing all day until finally Kurth had a sworn statement from each prisoner, countersigned by Koblenz himself. He was taking no chances that any of the prisoners might go back on his testimony later. Finally

Kurth extracted a statement from Captain Koblenz and the interrogation was over.

That day the statements were sent to the office of Major Moore, who belonged to the First Army's Inspector-General's Office. The unit of the 1st SS Panzer Division that had committed the atrocities in the Amblève valley and at the crossroads at Baugnez had been identified. Gradually these first pieces of written evidence would creep up the chain of command until finally they reached Eisenhower's Supreme Headquarters in Versailles. The first links between the future President of the United States and an obscure colonel in the German *Waffen SS* had been established. Soon Eisenhower would know that the man who had ordered the killing of his soldiers at the Baugnez crossroads was *Obersturmbannführer* Jochen Peiper.

NINE

The huge American 155mm cannon firing into La Gleize at close range from the next village of Stoumont shook Jochen Peiper more than any other gun he had encountered in five years of combat. Every time it fired it seemed to shake his very innards to pieces. He tried to control his jumpy nerves, but after four days in the trap of La Gleize with no sleep it was hard. Many of his young soldiers were in a permanent state of shock, too, jumping every time that damned gun fired, and Peiper knew they couldn't last much longer. Far too many of them were green teenagers, who had never visualized that combat would be like this. But divisional headquarters had still not radioed him permission to withdraw. If he were to save the 1,000-odd men left of his original 5,000 he needed that permission *soon*.

Unknown to Peiper, concerned for the welfare of his young soldiers, his corps commander, General Priess, had been trying to convince Dietrich, the commander of the Sixth Panzer Army, to let Peiper pull back. The matter had gone as far as Hitler's HQ, but in the end permission had been refused. Obviously Berlin still hoped that a link-up could be achieved with *Kampfgruppe* Peiper and that the drive to the Meuse could continue. For Peiper this was simply a pious hope and completely unrealistic. Not only were his men exhausted and burdened with several hundred casualties who filled the cellars of the ruined smoking village, but he was also virtually out of fuel. Once during the four-day seige, the *Luftwaffe* had tried to para-drop supplies of petrol to him, but most of the chutes drifted into the American lines. To the rear Skorzeny and his men disguised as Americans had managed to float some fuel to him along the river, but it was a mere drop in the ocean.

That day Peiper received a call to come to the sole radio capable of reaching across the hills to his rear, his only link with divisional headquarters. His hopes rose as he set off. Perhaps, now that they knew the *Luftwaffe* paradrop had been a virtual failure, they would let him withdraw from his untenable position in La Gleize.

He was disappointed. At the other end the strange impersonal voice, distorted by static, said, 'If *Kampfgruppe* Peiper does not report its supply position accurately, it cannot reckon on receiving a supply of fuel and ammunition. Six Royal Tigers ready for action east of Stavelot. Where do you want us to send them?'

Peiper flushed angrily as he picked up the mike. At divisional headquarters the Staff had absolutely no idea of his true position; they were all the same, these *'Etappenhengste'* (rear echelon stallions). 'Send them *via airlift* to La Gleize,' he snapped through gritted teeth. Then he pulled himself together and there was a note of pleading in his voice, as outside that damned gun pounded away. 'We must be allowed to break out immediately,' he said.

There was a moment's silence at the other end. Then General Mohnke – for now the Divisional Commander had come to radio – asked, 'Can you break out with all vehicles and wounded?'

Peiper's hopes soared. For the first time HQ was actually considering the possibility of a withdrawal. He said quickly, 'Last chance to break out tonight – without wounded and vehicles – please give permission.'

Mohnke was obviously not pleased with Peiper's reply. He didn't give a straight answer to Peiper's request, but he said he would take the matter up with the corps commander.

Peiper was satisfied. General Priess wouldn't fail him. He knew what it meant to be trapped. Hadn't he personally been besieged in Metz during the autumn for three months by the American Third Army? He doubled back to his HQ with shells exploding all around him and called an immediate conference of his surviving officers.

Confident that Priess would give him permission to do so, he told them they were going to break out of La Gleize. Swiftly sketching in their current position, he informed them that the nearest German units were somewhere on the other side of the River Amblève near Stavelot. Poking his finger at the map showing La Gleize, as the cellar shivered and trembled under the impact of the bombardment, he indicated the steep track that led down from the village to the river. There at the hamlet of La Venne (Wanne) there was gap in the American lines. Perhaps they would be able to slip through and cross the Amblève. His officers nodded their agreement. They all knew that their position here was hopeless. Now all they wanted to know was – when.

Peiper had his answer ready, even though he had still not received
permission. 'Tomorrow morning between two and three,' he replied.

Leaving them to work out the details, he summoned McCown to his
cellar. 'We have been called back,' he told the American, trying to hide
the seriousness of his position.

McCown forced a smile, though he was not exactly pleased at the
thought of the months he might now have to spend in a German POW
camp. Remembering that Peiper had promised him a ride in a Tiger
during their all-night conversation in the cellar, he quipped, 'Well, I've
always wanted a ride on a Royal Tiger'.

Peiper didn't tell his prisoner that they wouldn't be riding out of La
Gleize this Christmas Eve; they would be walking. Instead, he said,
'My immediate concern is what to do with the prisoners and my own
wounded.' He then suggested a solution. If he agreed to release all his
prisoners, except for McCown who would be kept as a hostage, would
he, McCown, guarantee that the US commander who took La Gleize
after it was abandoned release all the German wounded? Peiper would
leave behind the doctor of the Third Battalion, *Untersturmführer* Dr
Dittmann, to take care of the wounded, along with several captured
American aid men. Once the wounded had been released by the
Americans, he would return McCown.

The return of the prisoners was an important point of principle for
Peiper. He knew he could not break out successfully if he were
burdened with the wounded troopers. At the same time he knew that
the *Leibstandarte* had always prided itself on never leaving prisoners
in enemy hands if possible. The campaign in Russia had taught the
division that very unpleasant things happen to prisoners whose sleeves
bore the legend 'Adolf Hitler'. Twice in recaptured Russian towns they
had found their own men slaughtered by Russian NKVD troops. After
one such unpleasant episode in recaptured Kharkov, some units of the
division had taken to shooting their seriously wounded comrades
rather than abandon them to the Russian secret police.

McCown shook his head. 'Colonel,' he said, 'that proposal is a
farce. For one thing I have no power to bind the American command
regarding German POWs. After all you are not in a very good
bargaining position.'

'I know,' Peiper agreed. 'But I'd like to go ahead with the plan in the
hope that your commander will agree.'

McCown considered for a moment. 'All I can do is sign a statement
that I heard you make this offer. I can't do anything more.'

Peiper answered that this would suit him. Another captured US
officer, Captain Bruce Crisinger of the 823rd Tank Destroyer

Battalion, was brought in and the two Americans signed the statement that McCown drew up in English. This statement was then handed to Crisinger who would stay behind with the American prisoners soon to be released.

Thus one hundred and fifty Americans, all healthy and fit, were going to be left behind to take up arms once more in the near future by a unit which had allegedly caused mayhem and mass murder over the last week. Why hadn't Peiper ordered them to be shot and solved the problem they presented just like that? Was he really so concerned about his wounded who might well be shot out of hand by angry American troops, just as they had shot the captured SS men in Stavelot? Again questions without answers.

At five o'clock that afternoon Peiper was called to the radio again. His signals officer was crouched over the powerful *Luftwaffe* set asking urgently, 'Here is the main line of resistance. Where are the covering positions? May we break out? *May we break out?*'

Finally he raised divisional headquarters. A distorted voice crackled over the air waves, 'State when and where you will cross our lines?'

Peiper smiled wearily. They had done it. They could break out. But the speaker wasn't finished. 'You may break out, but only if you bring all wounded and vehicles,' he continued.

Peiper exploded with rage. 'Blow the damn thing up!' he yelled at the signals officer. *'Permission or not, we're breaking out of here on foot!'*

TEN

Between two and three o'clock on the morning of Christmas Eve, 1944, the surviving 800 men of *Kampfgruppe* Peiper started to slip down the track that led into the Amblève valley. As he joined his weary soldiers, Peiper knew he was beaten and the great counteroffensive in the west, the last of the Second World War, had failed. He was to have many years to consider what had gone wrong; why he had overlooked the necessity of the vital bridging equipment at the front of his column; why he had hesitated at Stavelot; why he had made so many mistakes in the boldest action of his whole combat career. But this freezing Christmas Eve he had little time for self-recrimination. He had to get his men away from La Gleize before the *Amis* realized the birds had flown.

By four in the morning they had sneaked away. Behind them the village lay in silence. In the cellars the US prisoners slept on, guarded by a handful of lightly wounded SS men who had volunteered to stay behind.

With a tremendous roar the first explosion shattered the pre-dawn silence. It was followed immediately by another, and another. Tank after tank, immobilized by lack of fuel, went up in flames. The last defenders of La Gleize, fifty in all, were destroying *Kampfgruppe* Peiper's heavy equipment. Green and red flares sailed up into the sky above the American lines. Up above, La Gleize was burning. God, the startled GIs asked themselves, what were the Krauts up to *now*? At the noise of the explosions Peiper allowed himself a wry smile and then he stumbled on, not far from where their sole prisoner Major McCown was, guarded by a young soldier with a drawn pistol.

Peiper was here, there and everywhere in the long weary column, forcing his young soldiers to keep going, sometimes with a quip, sometimes with a threat. He was not going to lose another man to the *Amis*. No one would fall out of his column.

McCown, himself very fit, was amazed at the pace Peiper set his exhausted men. It was murderous, with a mere five minutes' rest at the end of every hour to allow the exhausted men to catch their breath. Now and again the surgeon would hand out a few boiled sweets to give the soldiers a little extra energy and once he himself was given a sip of cognac to enable him to keep up, but that was all.

Dawn came late and they had still not reached the river. McCown realized for the first time that this was Christmas Eve. Soon his comrades, still at liberty, would be celebrating a traditional American Christmas, even if the turkey did come in cans. His would be probably spent in some lousy German POW cage, eating a lump of sour black bread and greasy sausage.

His face must have revealed his gloomy train of thought, for Peiper turned to him suddenly and pointed to a snow-covered fir tree, sparkling in the light of the ascending sun.

'I promised you the other night that I would get you a Christmas tree for Christmas. There it is.'

In spite of his weariness, McCown smiled. For all his toughness, Peiper was a typical German sentimentalist when it came to Christmas.

Some time later McCown caught up with Peiper again and pointed to eighteen-year-old Private Froehlich, who guarded him doggedly all the time with his drawn pistol. 'Can't you tell this guy to stop calling me "boy"?' he complained. 'After all, I am a major.'

'It's the only English he knows,' Peiper told McCown and turning to Froehlich explained what the major had said.

Froehlich nodded and said, 'Colonel, can't you get the Major to promise on his word of honour that he won't escape? I'm sick of holding this pistol up like this.'

Peiper translated the soldier's request and McCown said wearily, 'All right, I'll give you my word.' Froehlich put away his pistol gratefully.

At eight Peiper told his men they could take another rest. They flopped gratefully into the snow, gasping like old men. Peiper squatted on his haunches and considered his situation. They were not far from the river now, but its western bank would probably be held in places by the enemy. He would have to find that gap near Wanne; he could not risk a fight with the state his men were in now.

Suddenly he started and spun round. Shells had begun falling on La Gleize to his rear. Outlined against the white hillside, he could see the tiny black figures of American infantry going into the attack. The *Amis* still thought that he held the village.

Sprawled next to Peiper, a white handkerchief wrapped round his helmet so that he looked to Peiper like 'an umpire at a tactical exercise', McCown said sadly, 'Poor general. They'll fire him for this for sure.'

A little while later Peiper ordered the march to continue. He and a handful of staff officers hurried to the front of the column, while his NCOs got the exhausted soldiers to their feet. Wearily McCown got up too and waited, watching Peiper getting smaller and smaller in the distance as he prepared to lead his men through the last and most dangerous phase of this terrible forced march. Finally he disappeared into a wood, not far from the river, and McCown could see him no more. It would be the last he would see of the young German colonel for two years. When they met again, their roles would be dramatically reversed.

By nightfall the point of Peiper's column began to limp wearily across a small bridge over the Salm. Then they ran into trouble. The escapers bumped into retreating paras of the 82nd US Airborne Division. Tracer started to whiz back and forth among the fir trees. McCown didn't wait for a second invitation. As the alarmed SS scattered on all sides in the confused fight, he dropped to the snow. Mortars opened up. Bombs came hurtling out of the sky, exploding all around. Cautiously McCown raised his head. Froehlich was nowhere to be seen. He was on his own; this was his chance to escape. There were GIs out there somewhere. He started to crawl through the snow.

He covered a hundred yards, the front of his uniform soaked with snow, his face ripped and torn. Now he risked it. He stood up and, swallowing hard, began to whistle. Whistling as loud as he could, he set out towards the American positions. After what seemed an age, he heard an angry voice cry, 'Halt, Goddammit!'

He breathed a sigh of relief. He was among his own people once more. There would be turkey and all the trimmings for Christmas after all.

Peiper was at the end of his tether. After nine days without sleep, he had been slightly wounded in the skirmish in the woods, for the first time in his long combat career. He could not help himself any longer. He collapsed. He was carried the last few metres to the aid station that had been established at Wanne by the surgeon of the 1st SS Panzer Regiment. But he had made it. He had brought his 800 footsore, soaked, weary survivors back to receive a hero's welcome from their comrades. There he collapsed into an exhausted sleep, already recommended by General Mohnke for the Reich's highest award, the Swords to his Knight's Cross, even though he had failed to achieve his objective.

History does not record what Peiper's thoughts were that day. But he could have hardly realized that this day, 25 December, 1944, marked the zenith of his career, indeed of his whole life.

For some of us it is a dramatic event which signals that our life has changed irrevocably. The wounded soldier staring at the stump of his severed leg knows that from now on he will be a cripple. For most of us, however, the change does not come so dramatically. It is usually a simple process of ageing – being passed over for promotion in favour of a young man; the first discovery of a sagging chin; the discouraging realization that sexual power has gone for good. It is only when we look back that we realize that a particular day was a turning-point in our lives.

Such was the case with *Obersturmbannführer* Jochen Peiper. That Christmas Day, the last of the Second World War, he was only twenty-eight, but at the height of his military career, with the prospect of becoming the youngest general in the *Waffen SS* (soon he would be appointed the assistant divisional commander of the *Leibstandarte*). He was fit, virile, and supremely resourceful. Yet that day, unknown to him, marked the watershed in his career and his life. Already, as he slept his exhausted sleep, the enemy accountants in far-off Brussels and Versailles were beginning to assess the bill. All too soon now they would present the reckoning.

PART III

The Reckoning

'He lies like an eye-witness.'
Old Russian Saying

ONE

During that bitter winter of 1944–45 the Allies set about investigating the conduct of the *Leibstandarte Adolf Hitler* during the third week of December, 1944. The Belgians and the Americans proceeded separately. The former were concerned with the events which occurred in the Amblève valley; the latter confined themselves to what had happened at the Baugnez crossroads and during Peiper's drive to La Gleize.

For the Belgians the Prince Regent set up a commission of lawyers, professors and doctors to investigate the atrocities which had allegedly taken place between Stavelot and Stoumont. All that long, cold winter, when for the first time Belgium really started to know the pangs of hunger after a fairly easy four years under German occupation, the lawyers and doctors went from hamlet to hamlet taking statements from the surviving villagers. Late in April, 1945, with the Germans about beaten, already pushed back to their last defensive line on the Elbe, they published their report. It was entitled simply '*Crimes de Guerre*'.

The title was apt, for they had already made up their minds, without ever once being able to question any of the alleged criminals. The SS had committed wholesale murder in the Amblève valley. All in all, they estimated, Peiper's men had slaughtered some 300 unarmed civilians during the four or five days they had held the valley. The report is illustrated mainly by pictures of knocked-out German tanks. But there is one picture reproduced which shows a group of dead women, men and children, closely bunched together in what looks like the ruins of a shattered house. The caption reads, 'Bodies of civilians killed in the garden of House Legaye on the route between Trois Ponts and Stavelot'. The investigators' main informant about what happened there was Madame Gregoire, whom we have already met, and in due course she would be one of the star Belgian witnesses for the US prosecution at Peiper's trial.

There the matter rested. The committee had presented its report and that was that. Unlike the other Allied countries which felt that the Germans had committed crimes against their nationals, Belgium made no demand of the Americans, in whose custody Peiper would soon find himself, for his return to that country to stand trial for what appeared to be a major war crime. Why? Was it because the Americans would soon want him themselves to try him for similar crimes carried out against their nationals? Or was it because the Belgian authorities were not altogether convinced that the events in the Amblève valley had taken place exactly as the survivors had portrayed them to the committee?

Belgium was, and is, a curious country, made up of two bitterly opposed ethnic groups – the Dutch-speaking Flemings and the French-speaking Walloons. Not only that, there is a *third* ethnic group, which is perhaps the least known in Western Europe (even some Belgians do not know it exists). It is the 70,000-odd German-speaking community of the so-called East Cantons, centred around Malmédy, Eupen and St Vith.

Each group had long-standing differences from the others. The Walloons, who believed themselves the natural leaders of the country and who, prior to the Second World War, had made French virtually the sole official language, now felt the power slipping from their grasp into the hands of the Flemings. For their part, the Flemings had always been made to feel inferior to the Walloons. Although they contributed greatly to the prosperity of the little country, they rarely seemed to achieve any position of power. That appeared to be reserved for their French-speaking fellow citizens. As for the German-speaking minority in the East Cantons, who had become Belgian after the First World War in accordance with the terms of the Treaty of Versailles, they felt penalized by both the Flemings and Walloons. Their language was not recognized (it was only recognized as the country's third language in the 1970s), their infrastructure, roads, schools, etc, were little aided by Brussels, and they had virtually no say whatsoever in the political affairs of the country.

It is not surprising that German propaganda had played a great role in attempting to divide the three ethnic groups from one another and win them individually for the German cause. In the case of the Flemings, the propaganda began during the First World War when most of Flanders was occupied for four years by the German Army.

In the thirties, when the National Socialists came to power, this propaganda had intensified. Immediately after the occupation of Belgium in May, 1940, the Germans made determined efforts to destroy the central character of the country, with, it must be admitted, significant help from the ethnic groups themselves. The 70,000 citizens of the East Cantons immediately became German once more. Both Flemings and Walloons were invited to go to Germany to work in the booming war industry under very favourable terms, compared with those of the *Ostarbeiter* from the east who were compulsorily recruited and were little better than slaves. And while the Flemings were obviously racially much closer to the Germans, according to Himmler's crackpot theories, he did allow a large number of Walloon fascists, the *Rexists*, under their leader Leon Degrelle, to join the *Waffen SS*. In the end there was a whole regiment fighting in the ranks of the SS.

As for their ill-fated monarch, King Leopold, he remained in Brussels after the surrender. Unlike his two closest neighbours, the Grand Duchess of Luxembourg and the Queen of the Netherlands, both of whom fled into British exile, Leopold stayed on.

In short, in the winter of 1944–45, with Leopold now in Germany (whether he was forced to go there or whether he went voluntarily is still a matter of heated debate in Belgium), many of his subjects had uneasy consciences. Indirectly or directly they had collaborated with the Germans for four years and had made a good thing of it. Now the Western Allies had virtually won the war and the Germans were the enemy once more. What were they going to do?

It is obvious that many of them, knowing what was to come as soon as peace was declared, claimed that they had been in the Resistance or had suffered at German hands. But how could the nation as a whole be cleansed of the taint of having collaborated on a large scale? What could they use as a national alibi?

In September, 1944, they had welcomed the Americans with flags and bands and free drinks as their liberators. Three months later, when it appeared the Germans were returning, the photos of Churchill and Roosevelt which seemed to decorate every window disappeared in a flash. Even the black-marketeers wanted no more contact with Allied soldiers. In Spa, which had been the headquarters of the American First Army, the mayor was releasing imprisoned collaborators within an hour after the Americans had fled. Now the Americans, with some help from the British, had beaten the Germans after all. Surely the sufferings of the inhabitants of the Amblève valley would show the victors that Belgium had suffered for the cause, too?

How otherwise does one explain the fact that the investigating committee never took into account the constant bombardment of the roads in that area by American artillery? It was a barrage of such intensity that it stopped both Goltz's and Koblenz's columns. Nor was the fact that the valley was struck time and again by US dive bombers taken into consideration. Indeed, in nearby Malmédy, which was in American hands throughout the offensive, the US 9th Air Force caused more Belgian casualties in three air-raids than in the whole of the battle. Thereafter Colonel Pergrin's GIs called the US Air Force 'the American *Luftwaffe*'. Corporal Eliot's account of what he saw in the valley: 'Heads smashed in, men dismembered, pregnant women cut open' seems to fit in more with the results of bombing or shelling than the work of men armed with rifles and sub-machine-guns.

Where, too, are the eye-witnesses of the actual killings? Years later the author's own efforts to track down witnesses who had 'jumped out of a window' just in time or who had 'seen it happen through a hole in the wall' were unsuccessful. No one was actually present, save Madame Regine Gregoire, German-born and German-speaking.

At first, white-faced and obviously upset at being questioned on the subject, she was prepared to describe what happened in the Legaye house that December if I would come to her flat in Verviers a little later.

When I returned Madame Gregoire had gone. I was met by a strange man who explained, 'She could not possibly talk about the matter. It would upset her too much. Even TV violence gives her a bad head-ache.'

So that was that. Thirty or more years before, however, she had not hesitated at the trial to relive those events when they must have been much more immediate and traumatic.

Naturally, during the trial Peiper's men maintained stoutly that there had been Belgian partisans firing at them in the Amblève valley and this explained their own indiscriminate firing into civilian houses. Later, German apologists for Peiper wrote: 'The civilian population of Stavelot suffered severe losses from artillery fire from both sides. As, on the 18th, individual vehicles of the *Panzergruppe* followed, they were subjected to fire by civilians from numerous houses and 'In the attack of the tank group through Stavelot, civilians were found in the place, who were subjected to artillery fire from both sides. The mass of the follow-up vehicles were subjected to heavy fire from numerous houses by civilians'. Peiper himself told Monsieur Natalis, the schoolmaster at Stoumont: 'All you people here in this region are terrorists'. But he had to admit that he only came across one case of 'terrorism' personally. This was when armed Belgians threatened a wounded SS man left behind in Stavelot with their shotguns.

In Russia, and later in the retreat through France and Belgium, the SS had encountered partisans such as the *Maquis* and the Belgian *Armée blanche*. Indeed, one of Peiper's old comrades, the commander of the Hitler Youth Division, Kurt Mayer, known as 'Panzermeyer', had been captured by Belgian Resistance men not far from La .Gleize the previous September. But were there Belgian resistance workers actively helping the Americans in the Amblève valley? Had the SS any justification for indiscriminate shooting of civilians?

As we have seen there was much active and passive collaboration with the Germans in Belgium. But, of course, many Belgians were determined to resist the invaders of their country. However, any would-be Belgian resister back in 1940 faced a problem not present in neighbouring France. In France there were either large cities or great tracts of rough country in which men could hide. Not in Belgium. Although it was the most densely populated country in Western Europe, Belgium had few really large cities, apart from Antwerp, Brussels and Liège. For the most part the country is flat and without woods, with villages everywhere. There was one exception – the Ardennes, rugged, hilly, heavily wooded terrain, which was under-populated and close to the centre of Belgian communist resistance, Liège.

In September, 1940, Stavelot, thirty-odd miles from Liège and close to the new border with the Third Reich, became one of the first centres of resistance to the German occupiers. Using arms abandoned by the defeated Belgian Army in May, 1940, and buried in the Ardennes, the locals concentrated at first on an activity common to that whole border: smuggling. In this case they smuggled out French and Belgian POWs who had escaped from German camps. Two years later the local group went over to armed attacks on German soldiers, which only ended when a combined *Wehrmacht*-Gestapo operation rounded up many of the resistance workers in October, 1943.

Soon, however, a new group, modelled on the French *Maquis*, was set up in the area under a certain Emile Wolwertz and became a persistent thorn in the occupiers' flesh, earning Stavelot the title of '*Terroristennest*' (terrorist nest) from the local Gestapo unit stationed in Liège. In the summer of 1944, Wolwertz was killed in a gun battle with the Germans, but his unit fought on and aided the American 1st Army when it advanced to Stavelot in September, 1944. Some of the local *Maquis* even advanced as far as the Losheim frontier post, but there suffered a beating at the hands of the *Wehrmacht* and never again took part in regular military operations.

In September, 1944, the British authorities took over most of the civil administration of Belgium as far as civilian affairs affected the military, internal security, railways etc. Fearing that what was currently taking place in Greece might well happen in Belgium, too – namely that the communists would take over the whole of the Resistance and use it to seize power – the British ordered the *Armée blanche* to hand in their weapons. If they wanted to continue to fight against the Boche they could join the Belgian Army, currently being reformed and trained by the British Army.

On 18 November, 1944, the day set for the demobilization of the Belgian Resistance, a crisis arose in Brussels. The Resistance refused to hand in their weapons and threatened to call a general strike. Secretly, the British called in a whole division and surrounded the capital. But the threatened trouble did not materialize and the mass meeting of the Resistance on the subject of handing in their weapons went off without any major incident.

However, many weapons were not handed in and clearly the Ardennes area was an ideal place to hide these weapons until 'the day'. But were those weapons used against Peiper's men? We have already seen that a Belgian civilian spotted effectively for Major Hollis's gunners in Stavelot, but in the After-action Report of Hollis's 825th Tank Destroyer Battalion no mention is made as to whether this unknown Belgian was armed or not.

We *do* know, however, that during the cross-examination of the Belgian witnesses at the trial, one of them, Jean Elias of Trois Ponts, who had just testified that he had discovered fifteen bodies of civilians murdered by the SS, proudly claimed that he had later helped American troops to capture the nearby hamlet of Aisemont.

He was asked: 'Were you wearing American uniform at the time?' to which he answered in the affirmative. The Defence Counsel then asked:

'Where did you get the American uniform?'

'I got it from the Maquis.'

'What is the Maquis?' asked the Counsel, Dr Leiling.

'It is the Army of Resistance.'

'It is composed of Belgian civilians, is it not?' Leiling pressed home his point.

'Yes.'

Although the testimony elicited by Leiling did not speak of any mass activity by the Resistance in the Amblève valley, it did suggest that armed guerrillas had been operating in the area in the third week of December, 1944.

So how can one sum up the Prince Regent's committee's case against the Germans? The Belgians had obviously not taken into consideration the fact that a shell knows no difference between a soldier and a civilian, or between friend and foe. They might, too, have been motivated by a slight feeling of national guilt, which might have been assuaged by showing that their compatriots had been helpless victims of Nazi terror and that Belgium therefore had a rightful place in the victorious Allied camp. They had carried out their investigation in an atmosphere of charge and counter-charge, in confused circumstances, complicated by crowded hospitals, bombed and wrecked houses, mass graves and shocked survivors who were fighting for any means of staying alive that bitterly cold winter. They had no means whatsoever of finding out the German side of the story. Above all, they had refused to ask themselves that one crucial question: *How did Knittel's soldiers have so much time to go around shooting useless civilians when they were fighting for survival in the valley of the Amblève?*

TWO

On 14 January, 1945, officers of the 1st Army's Inspector General's office followed troops of the 30th Infantry Division, which had defeated Peiper at La Gleize, into the field south-west of Baugnez. Heavy snow had fallen there on 17 December and the field was covered by two to five foot of snow. At first it was feared that the bodies underneath the snow might have been booby-trapped, but examination showed they weren't and the black soldiers of the Graves Registration started digging.

As each dead body was freed, a numbered placard was placed on it and it was photographed. All the bodies were well preserved, due to the cold. They were taken down to bomb-shattered Malmédy and placed in a heated room where the macabre business of thawing them out began, so that they could be medically examined.

Most of them were found to have multiple bullet wounds in the face, chest, and abdomen. Some had wounds in the temple, forehead and, significantly, behind the ear. *Coup de grace* perhaps? Others showed further damage suffered after death, probably by shellfire. None of them had been robbed. Several of them still possessed money, watches and cigarettes. It was noted at the time that a 'considerable' number of the dead had been frozen with arms still raised above their heads. At least this was what was said at the subsequent trial.

A week after the exhumation SHAEF's Court of Inquiry opened at the US Military Hospital in the town of Harrogate in England. Under the presidency of Colonel Boraston of the British Army, the three judges on the bench considered the evidence, took further testimony and questioned witnesses (apparently twenty had survived whatever had happened at the crossroads).

Together with the statements later made by the captured SS men of

Peiper's *Kampfgruppe*, this is the picture that emerged. The survivors of the first brush with the SS from Battery B were joined by twenty other prisoners, including engineers, MPs, and two medical corps men from the 99th Infantry Division, Samuel Dobyns and Roy Anderson. In all it was estimated that there were 150 prisoners at the crossroads before the trouble started. By now the GIs knew who their captors were because one of the SS had laughed at them and had mocked, 'The First SS welcomes you to Belgium, gentlemen.'

A Panther rattled past and an officer standing in the turret called out cheerfully, 'It's a long way to Tipperary, boys'. The line from the British Army's marching song in the First World War meant nothing to the prisoners; their eyes were fixed on a self-propelled gun which was having difficulty in getting round the sharp bend. It was causing a minor traffic jam. When the jam was finally sorted out, two Mark IV tanks appeared and were manoeuvred into position so that they could bring their machine guns to bear on the prisoners. Their numbers were '731' and '732'. This meant they belonged to the third platoon of the 7th Company. The last digit identified them further. 731 was crewed by Sergeant Hans Siptrott as tank commander, Corporal Gerhard Schaeffer as driver, Private Arnhold as radioman and Corporal Wetengel as gunner, with Private Georg Fleps as his assistant. The last-named stood on the turret with a pistol pointed at the prisoners.

The second tank, 732, was commanded by Sergeant Clotten, but only two of his crew were ever identified. They were Corporal Koewitz and Private Vogt.

This information allowed the investigators to make certain deductions. The awkward self-propelled gun belonged to Major Diefental's battalion. He had already been identified by the US combat jacket he had looted. The SP and the Major had passed on, so he could not have been held responsible for what followed. Peiper himself, as we have seen, had already taken another route to Engelsdorf (Ligneuville), along with Major Knittel. This leaves Major Werner Poetschke, who commanded the main armoured element to which the 7th Company belonged, as the senior officer responsible for whatever occurred at the Baugnez crossroads.

Now the rear elements of the *Kampfgruppe* started to come down from Thirimont with the 3rd SS Engineer Company in the lead. The waiting prisoners saw an officer who they presumed was Poetschke confer with the engineer officer. Thereupon the latter strode over to Sergeant Siptrott in 731 and told him, 'The prisoners are to be killed and it must be done quickly. Everybody is needed up ahead and there is no time to waste.'

Siptrott protested, 'But I don't have much ammunition, sir.' The officer told him to do as he was told and Siptrott looked a Georg Fleps. Twenty-one-year-old Fleps was a so-called 'booty German', one of thousands of ethnic Germans from Roumania who had been recruited into the SS by Himmler's chief recruiter, General Berger, when the sources of German manpower, especially for the SS, had begun to dry up. His German was based on a medieval German dialect which his forefathers had taken with them from their native Swabia to Roumania in the Middle Ages. His personality was a little more emotional than that of his German comrades, and, as is often the case with those who join a major ethnic grouping to which they don't really belong, he tended to be more fanatical; 'more papal than the Pope' as the Germans say.

Raising his pistol, Fleps took aim and fired. The bullet hit Lieutenant Lary's driver who was standing immediately beside him. The driver went down, falling backwards and carrying with him several other GIs in the next rank. The GIs started shouting in alarm. Private James Massara, from Battery B, and the medic Samuel Dobyns immediately pushed their way through the startled ranks to the rear. Fearing that the men would make a run for it and bring down more fire on themselves, Lary cried out, 'Stand fast'.

Fleps fired again. A doctor standing next to Sergeant Ken Ahrens went down. Now someone cried out in German, '*Schlag sie tot, die Hunde!*' (Kill them, the dogs). Machine guns on both the tanks opened up, mowing the prisoners down. They fell in heaps, some genuinely hit, others reacting more quickly and throwing themselves down, pretending to be hit.

Methodically the German gunners worked back and forth until finally, according to Fleps, there was only one American left standing. This man he personally shot dead. At that moment the driver started the engine of 731 and Fleps was thrown off balance and hurt his leg.

Within five minutes it was all over. By about ten past two, as 731 started to move off down the road to Ligneuville, silence had returned and the field was littered with the bodies of dead and dying men.

But, as we know, all were not dead. Some had fallen singly, others lay in heaps as if in their extreme fear they had pressed together for protection. Now the survivors began to ask themselves if this was not the time to make a break for it. The two tanks had gone.

Among these men were Lary, wounded in foot and leg; Ahrens, shot in the back; Dobyns, wounded four times (he had been recommended in Normandy for having rescued a wounded German under fire); and Privates Massara and Reem, who had not been wounded at all.

But before they could make their escape, a new horror was inflicted upon them. Some of the SS engineers started walking down the ranks of the fallen, administering the *coup de grace*. If any showed signs of life, they had the back of their head blown off or their skull smashed in with a rifle butt. Private Jakob Weiss of the *Kampfgruppe*'s communication platoon, who had just arrived on the scene, testified later on oath that he saw one of the engineers testing whether the *Amis* were dead by kicking them in the testicles! He also testified to having watched an engineer pull the boots off a live GI, saying, 'You can go back to sleep now'. He then shot him in the head. Weiss also saw a Private Gustav Sprenger, then eighteen, kill five mortally wounded Americans with his pistol, laughing 'hysterically' all the while.

To Ahrens all the German killers seemed to be laughing. 'Maniacal,' Lary described it. Ahrens watched as a medic from Battery B, unable to stand the moans of the wounded man lying next to him, raised himself on one knee and plugged the man's wound with a first aid kit. A German engineer waited until he had finished, then cold-bloodedly shot them both. He, too, walked away laughing.

Lary heard a German approaching him. A pistol barked. The slug shattered the head of the man next to him. Lary waited for it to happen to him. '*Tot*' (dead), the German muttered and walked away, evidently thinking the young officer was already finished.

Now the firing started to die away and the survivors – officially they were listed as forty-four – waited as vehicle after vehicle rumbled by, heading for Ligneuville. Everywhere the men alive were whispering, 'Anyone else alive? Any of you guys still alive?'

Whispered responses came from all sides and they started to plan their breakout. In the end there seems to have been some twenty men who were either unhurt or not badly wounded and who wanted to have a go. Lary urged them to wait for darkness; it wouldn't be long. There were still German soldiers at the crossroads a few yards away. But the survivors had had enough of being living targets. It was Private Massara, still unwounded, who stood up first and yelled (surprisingly enough), '*Let's go!*'

They sprang to their feet and began to flee across the wet field in the general direction of Malmédy in the valley below. For a moment the Germans at the crossroads were too surprised to react. Then they opened up. Lary, going all out, saw one GI drop, but the rest kept on running.

Massara, Reem, Smith, Profanchik, Ford, Ahrens and three other unnamed men reached the woods, some two hundred yards behind the Café Bodarwé. Lary, Paluch and some twelve others swerved towards the café itself. Lary shouted a warning. They shouldn't go inside the place. Lary ducked into the same shed in which Ford had hidden earlier. Paluch and the others ignored his warning and went inside.

According to Lary the SS men dismounted a machine gun from one of their vehicles and called for the GIs to come out. They refused. Thereupon the SS set fire to the place and when the GIs tried to scramble out to safety they were mown down. At the back of the burning café, Sergeant Paluch and a few others played dead. But this time the German killers did not come looking for them. Under the cover of the smoke from the Café Bodarwé they managed to reach the woods and safety.

One of the witnesses, the wounded aidman Samuel Dobyns, told a slightly different story. Under cross-examination, he said that Fleps's pistol-twirling had caused one of the Americans to cry 'Stand fast!' It was at *that* point that Fleps had fired. He then fled and heard the machine-gun fire after he had run some distance. Under further cross-examination Dobyns agreed that other prisoners had broken ranks in response to the pistol shots, but *before* the machine guns had opened up.

Dobyns' testimony suggested that the crossroads killings had been nothing more than a tragic error. The trigger-happy Fleps had fired at the prisoners in a nervous reaction to a shout in a language he didn't understand. Later this interpretation was supported, in part, by testimony from other German witnesses. One SS man of the First Platoon of the Seventh Panzer Company said at the trial that his tank had stopped behind 'two or three other vehicles' when there was a sudden burst of fire from the vehicles in front. The sergeant in charge of his tank reacted immediately, firing some fifty rounds. No evidence of premeditation was contained in these witnesses' testimony. Naturally, however, it could be assumed that all these SS witnesses would be reluctant to offer testimony damaging to their comrades.

But in that last winter of the war no one was paying much attention to Private Dobyns' testimony and its suggestion that it had all been a tragic error. The SHAEF Court of Inquiry found it established 'beyond question' that a large number of Americans had surrendered. They had done nothing to forfeit their rights as POWs. Seventy-two of them had been killed in a manner 'unprovoked, deliberate and brutal'.

Now it had to be established whether, prior to the offensive, a general order had been issued by the Sixth SS Panzer Army to kill all prisoners. More importantly, the man who had commanded those killers *Obersturmbannführer* Jochen Peiper had to be found and made to pay for his crimes.

THREE

On 3 March, 1945, Peiper went into his last battle. As Assistant Divisional Commander of the *Leibstandarte*, he was to attack in Hungary and attempt to split the advancing Russians in two. Even such old hares as Peiper thought the plan, which was Hitler's, absurd. That day he reconnoitred the Division's jumping-off point in pouring rain. Ordering his driver to stop, he pointed to a vast morass of thick black mud, stretching eastwards as far as the eye could see, and said dramatically, 'We are now at the start line!'

Later that day he fought his way through the mud back to the divisional HQ at Veszprem, where he telephoned 1st SS Corps Headquarters. Angrily he shouted over the phone, 'I have tanks, not submarines! You can kiss my arse, but I won't do it.'

'Keep calm,' his Corps Commander replied soothingly. 'We're doing something about it.'

But nothing was done and by the middle of March it was obvious that last attack of the 6th SS Panzer Army was a miserable failure. Peiper, as usual, had made the deepest penetration. He was only twenty miles from the Danube, which was the Sixth's first objective, when Priess, his Corps Commander, called him and asked him what the devil he was doing so far ahead of the Sixth. 'Don't you know the Russians are attacking Vienna by now?'

In disgust Peiper retreated with his remaining twenty-five tanks, taking up a position astride the Budapest-Vienna highway. The spearhead of the Red Army followed him with such reckless abandon that Peiper was able to knock out 125 of the new Russian Stalin tanks without loss to himself.

Now the Sixth SS Panzer Army started to retreat in earnest. Here and there discipline began to break down. Army Commander General

Balck, no friend of the SS, spotted what he thought were SS men of the *SS Viking Division* fleeing westwards. He reported what he had seen to his superiors. In the general confusion another commander told Hitler, 'If the *Leibstandarte* can't hold their ground, what do you expect us to do?'

Hitler flew into a rage. He shouted at Field-Marshal Keitel, 'If my own *Leibstandarte* can't hold their ground, they aren't worthy of carrying my personal emblem.'

Thus the following message was sent to Dietrich: 'The Führer believes that the troops have not fought as the situation demanded and orders that the SS Divisions, *Leibstandarte*, *Das Reich*, *Totenkopf* and *Hohenstaufen* be stripped of their armbands.' It was the end of the road.

In the lower echelons of the Sixth SS Panzer Army the story went round that Dietrich had said he would rather shoot himself than carry out such an order and that he had sent his own medals back to the Führer *in a chamber pot*! He hadn't. Instead he kidded himself that Hitler had been misinformed.

Peiper could not take it as calmly as Dietrich. He called his officers together and told them angrily, 'Let's take a chamber pot, put all our medals in it and place the ribbon of the Division Goetz von Berlichingen around it.'

His officers knew what he meant. The name of the division was synonymous in German with 'lick my arse'. Angry as they were, the officers thought Peiper was going too far and prevailed upon him to drop the idea.

But the die had been cast. The Imperial Guard had broken with their Führer.

The last week of the war found the Sixth SS Panzer Army in Czechoslovakia, trapped on all sides. To the west General Patton's 3rd Army was advancing rapidly. The Red Army was pushing forward· from the east. The Czechs themselves were in full revolt.

By now Dietrich's Sixth was an army in name only. As the burly Commander commented with grim humour, 'The Sixth SS Panzer Army is well-named all right. It's only got *six* tanks!' This was an exaggeration but it did indicate the diminished state of what had been, at the beginning of 1945, Germany's most powerful armoured force.

In Prague the *Leibstandarte*, or what was left of it, was fighting a strange battle, fighting not only the Czech patriots but also the Russians of General Bunyachenko's Division, which up to recently had been in German pay. Now the Russian renegades had gone over to the Czechs in the hope that this might save them. It didn't. General Bunyachenko ended up on the gallows and most of his men found themselves in the Gulag. Finally the Czechs allowed the *Leibstandarte* to pull back towards Patton's Third Army.

One eye-witness account of that first meeting between the vanquished and the victor depicts a little scene which was typical of many others: 'There were the first Americans. Tall slim fellows with an Indian's head badge on their arms. "All big enough for the *Leibstandarte*", my friend Heinz remarked drily. Our commander was immediately surrounded by them. Suddenly a tall American grabbed at his Knight's Cross and tore it from his neck, laughing out loud. We jerked up our weapons, but our commander indicated we should lower them again. I shall never forget his face. Pride, contempt, sorrow were all reflected in it.

'This then was the end.'

This reaction seemed to have been typical of that of many of the more sensitive and intelligent SS officers. Apparently they thought that the Second World War would end like some nineteenth-century conflict with grave, dignified ex-enemies shaking hands before the vanquished leader handed over his sword to depart with his shoulders squared in gallant adversity.

But there were to be no Waterloos or Gettysburgs this summer. In the last few months some highly unpleasant details had come to light about the Nazi régime. Names like Buchenwald and Belsen loomed large. Tough old 'Blood and Guts' Patton had been sick after visiting a concentration camp. There was horrified talk of human bodies being boiled down for soap, lampshades made of human skin, terrible experiments carried out in living subjects, mass murder by the million. The Western Allies were in no way inclined to forgive. They wanted revenge.

Peiper, for his part, refused to surrender. With a few companions, all still armed, he set off for home. But he never reached it. Only a dozen miles from where his wife and three children lived in Bavaria he was captured by an American patrol. Like the rest, he went into the 'cage'. Later he recorded the shock of that event. 'As the world of barbed wired closed about us, we were children who had lost their mother overnight. We had been brought up under the clear rules of the front and we weren't capable of understanding the new rules of the game.... Our innocence was boundless. The state had taught its youth only how to handle weapons. We hadn't been trained in how to deal with treachery. Yesterday we had been part of the Greater German

Army; today we were scorned and avoided, surrounded by the howling mob as the whipping boys of the nation.'

In the years to come Peiper would learn just how innocent he had been in that summer of 1945.

The first real indication that Peiper had that he was not going to be regarded just as an ordinary POW came in August, 1945. That month he was taken by American MPs to the Third Army's Interrogation Centre at Freising, Bavaria. There he was cross-examined by a 'Mr Paul', who later turned up as Lieutenant Guth, which was probably his real name.

Mr Paul made it clear to Peiper, as the latter explained in his 1948 statement, that US Army investigations had given a 'surprisingly favourable picture' of him. Although he had been Himmler's adjutant, he had been the only one on the *Reichsführer*'s staff to have retained his personal integrity. His reputation, Mr Paul went on, as a good soldier and tank officer was not doubted and the Intelligence report made by Major McCown had shown his activities 'in a very favourable light'.

However, Mr Paul informed Peiper, the American people had been enraged by the events at the Baugnez crossroads and demanded a scapegoat. Somehow or other the US Press had managed to get hold of Peiper's name and now regarded him as the 'Murderer of Malmédy'. Indeed he was the most hated man in the States and 'the US soldier's public enemy number one'.

Paul suggested that, as Peiper's life was already forfeited, because (a) he had been Himmler's adjutant, (b) the Press had already pre-judged him and (c) he was a threat as the potential leader of some kind of Nazi Resistance movement, he should show that he knew how to lose and should admit that he had ordered the prisoners to be shot at Baugnez.

Peiper absorbed the information and told Paul, according to his own statement, that, 'I was prepared to take full responsibility upon myself on one condition – that not one of my subordinates should be tried on the same charge'.

Paul said he would consider Peiper's offer and there ended the first meeting between the future member of Captain Fenton's War Crimes Commission and the future 'war criminal' Jochen Peiper.

In early September, 1945, Peiper was transferred to the Oberursel Army Group Interrogation Centre, run by US Army Intelligence (the CIC). There he was placed in an isolation cell where he remained for seven weeks. Strangely enough, he did not find those seven weeks in solitary an eternity. As he wrote in 1952, 'Solitary confinement came as a kind of relief. One's nerves relaxed. Slowly one's fists unclenched and angry resentment against one's fate gave way a little.'

During this period Peiper was closely questioned about Major McCown who had been his prisoner in La Gleize. His interrogators were apparently not at all interested in the events at Baugnez. Starting off in a general way, they asked about the behaviour of the American soldiers he had captured. Had they collaborated in any manner? Then they started to ask specific questions about McCown's four-day captivity. Surprised at their interest, Peiper told them that McCown had behaved perfectly correctly and had revealed nothing of military importance to his captors. Finally his interrogators departed, leaving the prisoner wondering why the *Amis* were so interested in a man whom he had last seen nearly nine months before. It would be another six months before he discovered the reason.

It was during his period at Oberursel that Peiper first met the American who finally brought about his downfall, but who, twenty years later, was still writing to the 'war criminal' he managed to sentence to death. This was Major (later Lieutenant-Colonel) Burton F. Ellis from California. In civilian life he had been a lawyer specializing in divorce cases dealing with the sordid affairs of middle-class citizens of the Golden State and their petty suburban infidelities. Now, in his early forties, he was actively lobbying the Judge Advocate's Branch for permission to take over the 'Malmédy Case'.

The introduction was short and impersonal. To Peiper, Ellis looked like a typical 'rear-echelon stallion', as they called such soldiers in the SS. Indeed Ellis had come to Europe after the fighting was over. Such men, he told himself, could not understand the black-and-white thinking of the 'front swine' whose very lives might depend upon swift, straightforward, reactions and decisions. Ellis, for his part, must have thought Peiper a typical, hard-bitten, unrepentant Nazi.

That day Peiper was taken out of his prison for the first time. Guarded by heavily armed 'white mice', as the prisoners called their white-helmeted MP guards, he was driven in the car that followed Ellis and his interpreters to a little town called Bensheim an der Weinstrasse. Here (although Peiper didn't know it at the time) the four main witnesses at the coming trial were waiting for him: Ahrens, Ford, Dobyns and Lary.

Ellis told Peiper to get out of the car and, with his escort, he walked over to the waiting Americans. Intently the soldiers stared at the prisoner, wearing a nondescript *Wehrmacht* uniform devoid of any badges of rank. Ellis waited expectantly, but nothing happened. As Peiper wrote three years later, 'I was confronted with the American survivors of the Malmédy crossroads. Without success!'

Curtly Ellis ordered Peiper to get back into the vehicle.

Later, perhaps as some kind of punishment for the failed confrontation at Bensheim, Peiper was confined for twenty-four hours in what he called '*die Warmezelle*' (the 'warm cell'). At first it must have been pleasantly warm after the cold of his normal cell, but by the time the temperature had soared up to 40, 50, 60°C Peiper was sweating and gasping for breath. Now he realized that the *Warmezelle* was some kind of torture.

In the end he could stand the heat no longer. Grabbing a stool, the only piece of furniture in the cell, apart from the bunk, he started to break the window glass and smash the central heating system. The temperature went down and the next day he was taken back to his old cell. That was the one and only time that the team investigating the Malmédy Massacre tried physical torture on Jochen Peiper. Others were not so fortunate.

FOUR

If the American interrogators only tried third-degree tactics on Jochen Peiper once during the investigation leading up to his trial, they tried it many times on his unfortunate men. Throughout the summer of 1945 some 1,100 members of the *Leibstandarte* were interrogated. Of these, several hundred suspects or potential witnesses for the prosecution were imprisoned in the modern jail near Stuttgart at Schwaebisch-Hall. There each suspect was placed in a separate cell, often blacked-out. They were allowed no contact with the outside world, no legal advice, no exercise period, not even a visit from a priest or a parson. When the junior senator from Wisconsin, one Joseph McCarthy, found out that the prisoners were not allowed to see a clergyman, he exclaimed during the hearing on the conduct of the Malmédy trial: 'And you (John King, one of the guards at Schwaebisch-Hall) knew there was some sizeable number of Protestants, Catholics or Jewish boys! I understand then there was no chaplain assigned to these boys.' *Jewish SS men!*

The remark may have caused some amusement later, but there was nothing funny about the treatment accorded the SS prisoners from December, 1945 to April, 1946. They were subjected to the usual 'sweet-sour' technique beloved of professional interrogators, reinforced by the third-degree methods used by American police in the thirties and forties, which bordered, in some cases, on near-torture. In return for promised rewards – reduction of possible sentences, increase in food rations for themselves and their families outside (at this time rations for the average German were lower in calories than those of the Nazi concentration camps) – selected prisoners were asked to inform on their comrades. This was the 'sweet' technique. If they refused they soon learned what 'sour' meant. Punishments such as semi-starvation, threats to their families and mock hangings were tried on them. Often this interaction between kindness and severity worked, as is recorded in the statement made by twenty-one-year-old Max Hammerer from Peiper's former command who was later sentenced to death. On oath he stated in 1948, 'I had never seen a prison building from inside in my life before. As soon as I was admitted, accusations, curses, threats rained down on my head from all sides until I was totally confused. Soon I became a willing tool in the hands of the interrogators. If I said "yes" it became "no", and I had to write down "no". First Lieutenant Perl (a member of the War Crimes team) dictated my statement and, whether I wanted to or not, I had to write what Perl thought was right, although I knew it was wrong. This is how my statement in Schwaebisch-Hall came about. It is completely untrue and isn't mine, but that of the interrogation officer.'

Not all of the prisoners who later testified for the prosecution, and most of them were as young as Hammerer or younger, were so easily persuaded. As a consequence they were to suffer more, until the interrogators got the desired 'statement'.

SS Corporal Heinz Friedrichs was led into an underground room where his hood was removed. He found himself almost blinded by a bright light directed at his eyes. Narrowing them to slits, he could just see, behind the black-draped table, decorated by a crucifix, a rope noose swinging back and forth near the wall.

Two men were present, one a civilian named Harry Thon, the other an officer, William R. Perl, against whom the majority of charges of brutality would later be lodged. Short, balding and rather plump, Perl seemed an unlikely bully boy. Born in Prague, educated in Vienna, he had been a highly successful lawyer before the *Anschluss* of 1938 had forced him to flee. As a Jew, active in Zionist affairs, he knew what to expect when Hitler came. In the US Army he had worked on interrogating German POWs. This job took him to England and finally to the front. Here he had gained two battle stars, of which he was very proud, for having interrogated prisoners under fire.

Perl and Thon waited in silence until a third person took his place at the table – a 'priest' (in fact, one of the interrogation team so disguised to frighten the prisoner).

Then Perl began. He said to Friedrichs, 'So you are Friedrichs. We've been waiting for you for a long time. You can tell us anything you like, but we know you shot them down right and left.'

The terrified Friedrichs, who thought his last moment had come, did not know what to say. But before he could speak (according to his own statement) the two Americans began to beat him up. Still he protested his innocence. He said, 'I haven't killed any prisoners. If I had, I'd regard it as my duty to pay for it.'

Perl said, 'All right, let's tackle something else.' Leaving the Malmédy affair, he accused Friedrichs of having killed two Americans at the village of Stoumont.

Again Friedrichs denied the charge and was beaten for his pains, with Perl shouting at him, 'If you want to protect your officers, then you'll hang with them! But if you tell us everything, you'll be back with your parents in a couple of months.'

As Friedrichs continued to affirm his innocence, Perl changed his tactics: 'A democracy like America,' he said, 'is not interested in killing a young man like you, but if you persist, we'll put you in front of a court and have you hanged within twenty-four hours.'

Thereupon he turned to Thon, who was threatening that Friedrichs' parents would have their ration cards withdrawn in the morning (a virtual death sentence in that *Hungerwinter*, as the Germans called it) and said, 'One moment, Mr Chief Prosecutor. Perhaps Friedrichs is now prepared to confess.'

But Friedrichs wasn't.

Now Perl played 'sweet', while Thon played 'sour'. According to Friedrichs' statement, Thon grabbed him by the throat and slapped him about the face.

In the end he gave in. 'After they had treated me like that for an hour or so,' he said in his statement, 'so that I could hardly stand, I confessed to the untruth with which they accused me. I didn't care any more. In my apathy I wrote everything they told me to. I had to write a statement which was dictated to me by a first lieutenant I didn't know. This statement was used as the only piece of evidence against me in the Malmédy case.'

If some of Peiper's men were beaten into making their 'confessions', others needed only to be threatened, especially if they came from the east. They were told their families would be handed over to the Russians or the Poles, and they knew what that meant. Others were told that the ration cards would be taken away from their families, which amounted to condemning them to death by starvation.

But still the beatings and third degree tactics continued. In a statement made on 22 January, 1946, and witnessed by Captain Lloyd Wilson, a member of the US Corps of Military Police, ex-SS NCO

Erich Maute stated that on 6 March, 1946, he had been stripped naked in his cell and beaten up by Lieutenant Perl and two American soldiers. 'They hit me with their fists and kicked me. Later they used a wooden board. That afternoon they returned and asked me whether I was ready to confess. When I asked what I was supposed to say, since I hadn't done anything, they began to beat me again. They kicked me in the stomach and genitals so that I had to be sick. I collapsed in the corner and was dragged to my feet by the hair.'

That same month twenty-four-year-old Edmund Tomczak, a former private, was told by Perl and Thon that he was to be hanged; thereupon he was transferred to what they called 'the death cell'. At midnight on his first day there, Perl opened the door and announced in a solemn voice: 'Get ready. You are to be hanged immediately.' The door closed and Perl disappeared.

Ten minutes later he returned and told a shaken, white-faced Tomczak, 'You've got another twenty-four hours'.

Next morning Thon came into the 'death cell' and told the prisoner that his mother's ration card had been withdrawn and she was presently in Schwaebisch-Hall to watch her son hang.

This psychological torture went on for ten days. Then Thon and Perl appeared together and snapped, 'Get ready. Now you're finally going to be hanged.'

Thereupon, in Tomczak's own words, 'Someone pulled a black hood over my head so that I couldn't see anything. I was then taken out of the cell. By the changes in the direction – I was guided by two men – I noted that I was being led hither and thither. When we finally stopped, I was told, "You are now at the place of execution. There are already several men hanging on the gallows."

'Thereupon I was cross-examined once again, with the hood still over my head. All the same, I couldn't confess about events in which I didn't participate or know anything about. Either Lieutenant Perl or Mr Thon then said, "I'm going to count up to three. If you don't confess, you're going up!"

'By "going up", he meant hanging. A few moments later I was really hanging in the air and when I began to choke from lack of breath they let me down and asked whether I was ready to confess. These attempts at hanging were always signalled by the command "Hangman – *up*!" They were repeated several times.'

In the end Thon and Perl gave up on the obstinate soldier.

Sergeant Roman Clotten, who had been the commander of Tank 732, was placed in the 'death cell' by Thon in January, 1946. On the fourth of that month an officer appeared and began cursing Clotten.

After beating the German up, he told him that the only way he could save himself from immediate execution was to make a confession at once of what he had done at the crossroads.

'Cowed by this treatment and the threats, I wrote a report about the event that same evening. This report didn't seem to satisfy the interrogating officer. He insulted me in the meanest and dirtiest manner and threatened that I wouldn't leave the cell alive if I didn't write a confession and he was only prevented from striking me by the appearance of Mr Thon!

Mr Thon, playing the part of the honest broker this time, was friendly towards Clotten. 'He asked me where I came from and where my family lived. He told me that he came from the same area and promised to find out what had happened to my family, from whom I had not heard for over a year.'

'A few days later – I wasn't interrogated in the meantime – Mr Perl appeared and told me my wife and children had been killed in the last few days of the war. I had to accept this as the truth since I knew that heavy fighting had taken place in my home town. On that same afternoon I was taken to Mr Thon who told me to write my statement once again. He would dictate it to me. Thus I wrote the statement which was the basis of my declaration of guilt. This statement was the only piece of evidence produced against me in the trial. It was not confirmed by any other statement of evidence of other witnesses or accused persons.'

So ended the testimony of ex-Sergeant Clotten, one of the few persons actually identified as having been concerned with the events at the Baugnez crossroads.

By the end of April, 1946, the investigating team had obtained seventy-one sworn statements from prisoners, confessing to have shot some twenty individual American prisoners or Belgian civilians, plus general confessions about the murder of approximately *nine hundred American soldiers and Belgian civilians*! Thus it would appear that virtually every fifth man under Peiper's command had murdered a soldier or a civilian!

Now it was clear to the War Crimes team that the original investigation into the deaths of the seventy-one American soldiers found dead at Baugnez could be extended into a general accusation against the Sixth SS Panzer Army for having broken the rules of Land Warfare. As a result Generals Dietrich, Priess and Kraemer were informed that they would also be going up for trial. All in all seventy-three SS men of all ages and ranks would be tried. In order to simplify matters, 'to preclude the possibility of legal complications', as the order of 26 April, 1946, put it, they were formally discharged as prisoners-of-war. Now they became civilian internees, who were not protected by the Geneva Rules applying to POWs; yet they were to be tried by a military court-martial!

FIVE

Who were these men who, if we are to believe the prisoners' statements, bullied and tortured the Nazi elite into submission? Who were Lieutenant Perl, Mr Thon, Mr Paul, Captain Schumacher and the rest of the War Crimes Team who had forced the pride of the SS, *die Leibstandarte*, to talk, to break them down so that in the end they were not only confessing to every crime under the sun, but denouncing each other by the dozen? And what can we say of their methods which seem so brutal, even sadistic, forcing at least one prisoner to commit suicide?

In a cruel jingle of the time they were characterized thus:

> From Afric's shore, from Colomb's unscorched strand,
> Urgent there streams an eager Hebrew band,
> Imbued with our desire to serve the aims,
> Of Allied justice, see them stake their claims,
> To jobs in Germany. *They* know the ropes,
> And *their* control will answer all our hopes.
> Let us but serve and we will prove our worth,
> Till Hitler came and rudely thrust us forth.
> We helped the men who laid the powder train,
> So you can trust us not to help again.

This frankly anti-semitic jingle explains who they were – Jews who had been forced to flee from their native country, Germany, by the Nazis simply because of their religion. There had been Jews in Germany, of course, since the early Middle Ages. They had helped to form Bismarck's Empire in 1871, financed its expansion and the industrialization of the new Reich and fought in the trenches with their fellow Germans in the First World War. More than any other Jewish community in Western Europe, save in the United Kingdom, they had felt themselves at one with their non-Jewish neighbours. Then Hitler came to power and abruptly they became third-class citizens, their stores and services boycotted by their fellow Germans, their presence unwelcomed in places of entertainment, cafés and restaurants. As the new signs which appeared everywhere after 1933 maintained, Jews were undesired – '*Juden unerwunscht!*' New racial laws were promulgated which made it a punishable offence for a Jew to have sexual relations with a Gentile, and everyone knew the picture of a German woman, surrounded by grinning taunting SS men, a placard hanging round her neck saying, 'I have had sexual intercourse with a Jewish lout!'

They were fired from government jobs, forced to resign their commissions in the armed services* and allowed as doctors, dentists, lawyers, etc only to deal with Jewish clients.

Often enough in their long history the Jews have suffered persecution. In every European country from England to Spain, and notably in the nineteenth century in Russia, they had suffered, but never on such a scale and in such a clinical manner as in National Socialist Germany, where the Jewish community had been regarded by other Jews as more German than Jewish. The Russian pogroms and the medieval massacre of Jews in such cities as York, for instance, had usually been spontaneous outbreaks of greed, envy and popular brutality. At regular intervals the Jews would be slaughtered under the pretext that they were the race which had murdered Christ, the blood-thirsty locals conveniently forgetting that Jesus himself had been a Jew. The National Socialist persecution of the Jews was icily scientific, organized on a national basis and from the top. The Jews, it was stated, had been the cause of all Germany's ills since her defeat in the First World War. In the brutal terminology of the time they were '*Volksschadlinge*', national parasites. Within a matter of years those Jews who hadn't already heeded the warnings of *Mein Kampf* found themselves hated outcasts in their own country. Abandoning country, fortune and way of life, allowed only to take a pittance with them, often having to buy their way across Germany's frontier, sometimes being fed castor oil to check whether they had not hidden diamonds in their stomachs, they sought a new life elsewhere. But at the height of the Great Depression, with millions unemployed, where could they go?

* One notable exception was F. M. Milch of the *Luftwaffe*, who was protected by Goering.

In 1940, when Hitler invaded the Low Countries and France, they fled again, this time, if they were lucky, across the Atlantic. Here they were often unwanted too. With thirty million unemployed in 1939, these 'Americans of '39', as they were cynically named by American anti-Semites, weren't needed. There was an outcry from labour leaders at allowing more workers into the country. Other organizations such as the Ku Klux Klan spoke out against them. 'The European refugee poses a greater threat than the Negro,' Imperial Wizard Hiram W. Evans explained. 'The Negro is not a menace to Americanism in the sense that the Jew . . . is a menace.' Such demagogues as the radio priest, Father Coughlin, found a willing response among the millions of listeners, many of whom saw these 'Americans of '39' as a threat to the Anglo-Saxon racial purity of the United States.

But, however reluctantly, they were absorbed and, in due course, the younger of these refugees went into the Army after Pearl Harbor, and if we are to believe US novels about the American wartime Army, such as *The Naked and the Dead*, *The Young Lions*, and *From Here to Eternity*, they encountered anti-Semitism there too.

These, then, were the men who had returned to Germany with the victorious US Army to seek retribution on the nation that had forced them to flee their homes and plunged them into a new and uncertain existence. It is not surprising that they hated the Germans, especially those whose uniform had borne the same terrible insignia, the runic silver SS and skull and crossbones, as those who had killed millions of Jews in the concentration camps.

Belonging nowhere, neither to their 'homeland' nor to their newly adopted country, they were isolated in an Occupied Germany where their American comrades were making a full-time business of sleeping with the 'frowleins', the women of the enemy they had been busy killing the previous year. Cut off, frustrated, and angry at the way the average GI so speedily forgot the Nazi crimes, they obviously felt that no method was too cruel or too underhand to force a confession out of Hitler's elite, these former *Herrenmenschen*, the living symbols of Nazi arrogance.

Now, after a long hard winter of trying, they could present Lieutenant-Colonel Ellis with what they confidently believed to be an open-and-shut case against the accused SS men. They had four American eyewitnesses to the events at the Baugnez crossroads: Ahrens, Ford, Dobyns and Lary. They had several Belgian witnesses from the Amblève valley, notably Madame Gregoire, and a good score or so of SS men who would testify against their former comrades for the prosecution.

They had made no attempt to find independent witnesses, such as Madame Bodarwé or Henri Le Joly. They had not bothered to look for a reason why seventy-one Americans had allegedly been shot by Peiper's men at Baugnez where they presented no danger to Peiper, while in La Gleize, where his prisoners *did* present a threat to his escape plan, he allowed 150 prisoners to remain alive. The whole prosecution case thus rested on the testimony of American and Belgian eye-witnesses, supported and confirmed by the statements obtained from the SS men at Schwaebisch-Hall. This, and the fact that public opinion in 1946 was very definitely anti-Nazi, must have made the ex-divorce lawyer from California feel he simply couldn't lose.

But what of Jochen Peiper? His initial meeting with First Lieutenant Perl was at the Zuffenhausen camp for suspected war criminals in November, 1945. According to the statement that Peiper made to his lawyer in 1948, Perl told him then that the American public wanted his head. Unfortunately for Peiper, among those who had died at the crossroads were the son of a US senator (untrue) and the son of an influential American industrialist. The two bereaved fathers were out for his blood and were making a political issue of the matter. Peiper had to be punished.

The consequence, according to Perl, was that the US Press had already hanged him – in print. Perl, as Peiper told his lawyer three years later, admitted that he thought the German was a most unusual soldier, who was idolized by his subordinates. But he warned Peiper not to overlook the realities of his situation. His time was past; it would never come again. If we are to believe Peiper's statement, Perl was very honest with him. He said that the fact that the Germans had lost the war was their real crime and the question of personal guilt was purely secondary. Perl gave Peiper his word that he, Peiper, would never be freed. Soon, Perl told him, the Nuremberg Court would rule that the SS was a criminal organization. At present the *Waffen SS* was protected by the Rules of Land Warfare but, in Perl's opinion, the Malmédy trial would ensure that they would no longer be protected by the Hague Convention. So, Perl continued, Peiper should accept the inevitable and face up to the situation as befitted a Prussian officer.

Peiper asked Perl what he meant by this. Perl answered that Peiper's soldiers idolized him and believed that he was prepared to accept total responsibility for the crimes they had committed.

After some consideration, Peiper accepted this point of view. Perhaps he was flattered. Perhaps the suggestion appealed to a kind of Wagnerian death-wish. But all the same, he said, he wanted an American and a German lawyer present when he admitted his personal responsibility.

According to Peiper, Perl flushed with anger and said, 'If you go back to your cell now and commit suicide, leaving a note to say that *you* gave an order to shoot those men and that you are the real guilty party, I'll deny it in front of the Court and maintain you had nothing to do with the killings. The Führer's loyal *Leibstandarte* is not going to get away with it that easily!'

With that Perl stamped out, leaving Peiper to his thoughts. They weren't pleasant. As he was to record in that statement of 1948: 'The question of personal guilt or innocence is not important here and as far as the future is concerned, irrelevant. They (the Americans) can't let us out anyway because we know too much about their methods now. I don't think we shall ever appear before a regular court of law. My guess is we'll be eliminated in quick time with no member of the general public being allowed to be present at the tribunal.'

Thereafter Peiper was incarcerated in his lonely cell in the basement of the building, with hardly any light and food every two days. For three weeks he was not allowed to wash or shave himself. His sanitation consisted of an old chipped bucket in the corner, and there was no heat. It was in this manner that he spent his first peacetime Christmas and his thirty-first birthday, hungry, dirty and cold – a man who had once been featured on the front cover of *Signal* magazine and other National Socialist publications; who had been received by the Führer himself with the traditional clasped hands; who had been the darling of the SS, winning virtually every military honour the Third Reich could award. They had even sold postcards of him in the streets as if he were a film star! Now he lay rotting in a cell, a man condemned in advance to death. It seemed like the lowest point of his life. But there was worse, much worse, to come.

In March, 1946, Lieutenant Perl presented himself once more and told his prisoner, 'A lot has changed since our last meeting. Threatening clouds have begun to form over your head.'

Peiper asked him what he meant. Perl replied that all Peiper's former comrades, officers and men, had confessed. Not only that, but Generals Dietrich, Priess and Kraemer had done the same. He, Peiper, was the only one who had not admitted his guilt. Perl added menacingly, 'If you don't confess now, I'll be forced to use other means.'

Peiper waited tensely. Perl threatened to deliver Peiper's wife and children into Russian hands; after all the Russians thought him a war criminal, too, and would take appropriate revenge on his children.

Peiper forced a laugh. 'I think you are too good a psychologist,' he said, 'to make the elementary mistake of believing that I am a medium for threats of that kind.'

Perl changed his tactics. Calmly he told the prisoner, 'We know that you had nothing to do with the crossroads. We don't want you. We want Dietrich,' and with that he left.

The next day Peiper, who was now with the rest of his former comrades at Schwaebisch-Hall, was marched into the interrogators' office where he was told that a clause had been found in the Sixth Army's operating instructions for the attack in the Ardennes, stating that in certain cases captured prisoners would be shot. Perl paused before delivering the punchline, then came out with it. Seven or eight of Peiper's own officers would confirm this clause. Thereupon the door to the office opened to reveal several of his former officers standing there a little shamefaced and embarrassed.

Peiper broke at last. Once, each officer-cadet at Brunswick or Bad Toelz had been awarded a silver dagger at the end of his training, engraved with the legend '*Meine Ehre heisst Treue*' (my honour is my loyalty). It was a motto which had dictated their lives for years. Now the men who had once carried that same dagger were betraying him.

As Peiper wrote later, 'I began to doubt my own memory and experienced the feeling that I was in the labyrinth of a lunatic asylum. *Honourable tradition and pride in one's caste had been sacrificed for a cigarette end!*'

Perl piled on the agony. He produced affidavits sworn by Dietrich, Kraemer and Priess. Looking at the signatures which he had known for years, Peiper recognized them as genuine. Each affidavit confirmed the order.

Then Captain Gruhle, once Peiper's adjutant, was brought into Perl's office. He, too, confirmed that there had been such a clause in the operational orders, although he tried to soften his betrayal by stating that, as regimental adjutant, he would probably have been more familiar with the clause than his commander. Others followed, not looking at their former chief, and did the same.

Peiper capitulated. At Perl's dictation he began to write out a confession stating that there had existed an order allowing for prisoners-of-war to be shot in certain cases.

Thereafter things moved swiftly. As Peiper himself said later, 'From this time onwards the whole process left me completely cold. My belief that comradeship had been the only thing of value rescued from the bankrupt mess of the war was shattered. I felt a deep physical and psychic disgust for my adjutant, Mr Perl and my whole environment.

Peiper let everything happen to him numbly. A Sergeant Hiller confessed that in his presence, Peiper had ordered him to shoot two American prisoners. Peiper didn't hesitate. He signed the prepared statement agreeing that he had given the order. Some days later he was told that the former head of his *panzergrenadiere* and comrade of long standing, Major Diefenthal, had confessed to ordering prisoners to be shot at La Gleize. Again Peiper accepted the responsibility. He signed the statement maintaining he had commanded Diefenthal to do so.

'One killing more or less doesn't matter, eh?' Perl commented with one of his rare smiles.

When Sergeant Wichman admitted killing US prisoners at Ligneuville, Peiper immediately accepted the responsibility for having ordered him to do so. When Doctor Sickl, the regimental surgeon who had fed him candy on the daring breakout from La Gleize, confessed, Peiper accepted the responsibility again. He signed confession after confession. As he summed it up, 'I soon became renowned for my casual acceptance of responsibility. Twenty statements more or less meant nothing to me. If they had so desired, I would have accepted responsibility for the order at the crossroads.'

In the first week of May Colonel Ellis, the prosecutor, firmly convinced that he had a cut-and-dried case against the accused, now that he had the 'statements', rather foolishly went to visit Peiper. Peiper recorded the conversation as being 'on a personal, human plane . . . fundamental'.

Perhaps Ellis felt he could afford to be generous to the man who he was soon going to have sentenced to death. At all events he allowed himself to be drawn by the prisoner down a very dangerous (for him) path. Quietly Peiper asked him 'whether *he* personally really believed all things of which I am accused'.

As Peiper later told the court in front of a highly embarrassed Ellis, whose objection to this testimony had been overruled, 'I told Colonel Ellis that he surely would know that all my testimony resulted only from the fact that I wanted to save my men.'

'Whereupon Colonel Ellis had said, "I admire you and I hardly know another soldier who I estimate as highly as I do you. But you are sacrificing yourself on an ideal (sic) which no longer exists. The men whom you today think you have to cover up for are bums and criminals. I'll prove that to you in the course of the trial. We are now parting as friends and when we see each other again before (the Court) (it will be) as enemies and I'll have to paint you in the worst colors, but you'll understand that I will only be doing my duty."'

Strange as it seemed that a chief prosecutor in a major war crimes trial should be expressing his personal admiration for one of the chief accused, even hinting that he knew Peiper was innocent, it would mean nothing at the trial. Colonel Ellis was out for a conviction, and would let nothing stop him obtaining it.

PART IV

Trial at Dachau

'To hell with the truth! As the history of the world proves, the truth has no bearing on anything.'

Eugene O'Neill

ONE

Fittingly enough, the trial of the SS, or the 'Malmédy Trial', as the Press soon entitled it, was held at Dachau, some fifty miles from Munich. The town had once housed one of the oldest Nazi concentration camps and had been the scene of some of the greatest horrors of the Second World War. Now the dreary wooden huts that had imprisoned the pyjama-clad victims of the Nazi terror were to be used to try the men who had worn the same insignia as the brutal guards who had run the camp.

But now the roles were reversed. The victims, in this case the Belgian and American witnesses, were lodged in the villas once inhabited by the SS guards, while the seventy-three accused were imprisoned in the cell block of the former concentration camp's bunker. Not far away, in Cage III, Block 202, fifty-four of their former comrades who would testify against them were accommodated separately. The trial itself was to be conducted in Court B, a low wooden barrack block which had seen nearly a year's service as the place where the US authorities held most of the war crimes trials.

On 16 May, 1946, Court B was crowded as never before. Movie cameras whirred and flash bulbs exploded as the tall immaculate MPs in their white helmets started to lead the defendants in, under the command of the US Provost Marshal. A couple of them hobbled in awkwardly on crutches, but most of them were erect, slim and pale, the officers neatly attired in grey-green *Wehrmacht* uniforms, devoid of the insignia of their former rank. Amid the chatter and noise of the cameramen jockeying for position, the SS took their places on the raised wooden benches in their little cage, each of them bearing, for better identification, a white cloth with a black number on it. Alphabetically, first was Valentin Bersin, who became Number One and lent his name to the official title given to the trial – 'US versus Bersin'. Sepp Dietrich's number was 11, Priess was 45, Kraemer was 33 and Peiper was 42.

There exists a picture of Peiper taken that spring morning. It shows him neat and contained in his *Wehrmacht* tunic (though it didn't reveal that he was wearing GI combat boots several sizes too large for him), his hair brushed back, his hands clasped together and his jaw clenched so that one has the impression he is about to jump from his seat and shout a protest at the awful injustice about to be done to him.

The defence's German lawyers were there already: Doctors Hertkorn, Leer, Leiling, Pfister, Rau and Wieland, clad in their black robes, strange square-shaped hats and winged collars, so that they looked a little like Scottish ministers of the kirk. The men they had to defend had little faith in them. They were Germans, members of a beaten race and this was the 'court of the victors'. Besides, most pre-war German advocates had been members of the Party. If these men were allowed to practise by the *Amis*, it meant that they had safely emerged from the official process of de-Nazification. Could such men be trusted to represent SS men?

There was one other lawyer present on the defence team, heading a group of military advocates, who was even more unfamiliar with the defendants' case than their German lawyers. For, like them, he had had no time to prepare his defence. He was a tall, slim, sharp-featured American, soft-spoken and courteous, from Atlanta, Georgia, and his name was Colonel Willis M. Everett Jr. After six years in the Army he had just been assigned to Europe, where he had anticipated being given a non-legal role in US Military Government, but, to his horror, he, who had had little court-room practice, had been given the task of defending these killers. But soon he would come to identify himself with these unknown SS men to such a degree that he would make it his life's work to see that they were freed.

Everett knew, of course, that his 'clients' must think little of him. They saw in his presence yet another aspect of their American captors' sanctimonious subscription to so-called democracy. Indeed some of them, like Peiper, felt that the whole trial was simply a farce and believed that the *Amis* were mocking them by allowing an *Ami* lawyer to defend them. They were in for a surprise.

The court rose as Brigadier-General Dalbey entered, followed by seven field-grade officers, including Colonel Rosenfeld, the court's legal adviser. He, together with Colonel Ellis, would become the man most hated by defendants in the days to come. With the ease that comes of long practice, Brigadier Dalbey announced at exactly ten o'clock, 'This court is now open'. The Malmédy trial could begin.

Colonel Ellis began the proceedings by reading out the charges against the defendants: 'That the accused, charged as being parties concerned, did willfully, deliberately, and wrongfully permit, encourage, aid, abet and participate in the killing, shooting, ill-treatment, abuse and torture of members of the Armed Forces of the United States of America and of unarmed allied civilians.'

Most of the rest of the day was taken up by the prosecution reading out the charges, which were then translated into German. They weren't pleasant, even when uttered in cold official tones: '*Lined up against a wall and mown down with a machine-gun ... skulls beaten in by rifle butts ... taken out into the garden and slaughtered one by one.*' Yet the faces of the accused showed little emotion, neither fear nor remorse. To the Press they looked like a typical bunch of 'hardened SS killers', although at least two of the accused had been all of sixteen at the time of the alleged offences.

When the charges had been read, each of the accused rose to his feet and made the same plea: 'Not guilty'.

The formalities over, Ellis rose to his feet once more and opened his case for the prosecution. He told the court that some of the *Leibstandarte* men were ordered to 'excel in the killing of prisoners as well as in fighting. . . . Others were told to make plenty of *Rabbatz*, which in SS parlance means to have plenty of fun killing everything which comes in sight. . . . Others were told to bump off everything that comes in front of their gun.'

Ellis evidently believed his words, but he was well aware that he had very few eye-witnesses to back up his case against the SS. Basically his case rested on the statements made at Schwaebisch-Hall and he took care to point out to the court that some of his own prosecution witnesses might well go back on their original affidavits. Obviously he thought he had made a clever tactical move, for in a photograph taken of him just then he is smiling broadly, as if well pleased with himself.

Coming to the details of his case, Ellis started to introduce the SS witnesses who had agreed to testify against their former comrades. This part of the trial would take three weeks. Four of Peiper's former soldiers stated before the court that their commanding officer had told them on 15 December, 1944, 'to drive on recklessly, give no quarter and take no prisoners'. (As will be remembered, just before the offensive the *Leibstandarte* had helped to clear up the mess after the Allied air raid on Dueren.) Thus a Corporal Ernst Kohler stated that his platoon had been told, 'Avenge the lives of our women and children. Show no mercy to Belgian civilians. Take no prisoners.'

Three of Peiper's junior officers then testified that their former subordinates' statements were correct. One of them, ex-Lieutenant Tomhardt, said, 'I told my men that they were not permitted to take prisoners. Then I told them that they were not to shoot any prisoner of war who waved his helmet.' (This was a reference to Skorzeny's disguised commandos who were to use the raising of the helmet as an identification signal to friendly troops.)

The officers were followed by Corporal Gustav Sprenger who stated that when he had gone into the tiny church at La Gleize to help a wounded comrade, he saw a hundred American soldiers lined up across the square in the schoolyard, below which Peiper's HQ was located. A few moments after he entered the church, he 'heard a great deal of shooting from the direction of the school'. Later, when he emerged from the church, 'American soldiers were lying on the ground. Dozens of Americans, shot in sheds, against the cemetery walls and wherever they had been captured'. Sprenger completed this picture of mass slaughter by confessing that he and some others had come across two Americans carrying a wounded comrade on a stretcher. His pals had shot the first two Americans and he had killed the one on the stretcher.

Ellis gradually built up his case against the accused, allowing the Germans to incriminate themselves, playing off one SS against another. But this was the trial of the whole of the *Waffen SS*, and not merely a handful of sadistic young soldiers. Ellis was determined to involve the Sixth SS Panzer Army's senior officers too. Calling Sepp Dietrich, no longer his former swaggering self, to the stand, Ellis made him admit that, at a conference with Hitler at Bad Nauheim on 11 December, 1944, the Führer had issued a spoken command for a campaign of terror in the Ardennes. 'The Führer said he would have to act brutally and show no human inhibitions,' Dietrich said. 'A wave of fright and terror should precede the attack and enemy resistance had to be broken by terror.'

Asked by Ellis why he had made no provision for prisoner-of-war cages, Dietrich was perplexed. The prosecutor then said that at Dietrich's conference on 12 December, one of his officers, thinking that he had overlooked the matter, had asked, 'And the prisoners? Where shall we put them?' Dietrich had replied. 'Prisoners? You know what you can do with them.'

What did he mean by that 'Pontius Pilate kind of reply', Ellis asked.

Dietrich answered that he had meant that the Hague Convention was to be respected. No one believed him, particularly because the Sixth had apparently not provided any POW cages. He might have pleaded in his own defence that the Sixth was an assault army and prisoners could be directed to the rear, as in 1940. But he didn't. In the event the Sixth took some 7,000 American prisoners, all of whom arrived safely in the Reich.

While Ellis piled up the evidence against the accused, the defence lawyers, who had been barred from access to the 'statements', remained silent, especially Everett, who was virtually unprepared and was only now learning from the prosecutor's case what exactly his grim-faced clients were charged with. Once Everett rose and requested that the accused might be divided into three groups – officers, NCOs and enlisted men. Presumably he hoped this division might strengthen their resolve. But Ellis wouldn't have it and made a melodramatic plea against any change in the existing order of the trial.

'The defendants are together as joint perpetrators of the Malmédy and other massacres,' he told the court. 'Each defendant was a cog in a giant slaughter machine. They are asking for severance simply because the teeth of the machine meshed less smoothly when they were dripping with blood than when they were lubricated with the oil of victory!'

Whatever that statement meant, it had its effect. Colonel Rosenfeld, the legal officer, who consistently seemed to favour Ellis and who made all decisions concerning points of law, ruled that there would be no division of the accused and that was that.

Satisfied that he had got all he could out of the German witnesses for the prosecution, Ellis now produced the 'stars' of his case – the American and Belgian eye-witnesses. As was fitting in a military court, the officer came first. Virgil Lary, the ex-Lieutenant who was now a twenty-three-year-old student at the University of Kentucky, told the court, 'I heard two machine guns open up on the group. The firing seemed to become more intense. Those who were not killed originally fell to the ground. I fell with my face in the mud, my feet pointed toward the road.'

He was asked if he had heard any noises after the firing had ceased. 'I did,' he replied. 'I heard agonizing screams from the American wounded.'

'Anything else?' Ellis asked him then.

'Yes,' Lary answered. 'I heard single shots which sounded like they came from pistols.'

Lary admitted that he had not seen any Germans come into the field because his face was in the mud and his feet were towards the road where the Germans were.

'After the pistol shots,' he was asked, 'did the moaning and groaning cease?'

'Yes, completely.'

Lary's testimony had its effect. The picture he painted of laughing SS men finishing off the helpless wounded lying in the mud could not fail to turn the panel against the prisoners. Meanwhile Lary was invited to point out the man who had fired the first pistol shot into the prisoners. This was the highpoint of Lary's testimony at Dachau and he knew it. He took his time searching the faces of the Germans. Finally, pointing slowly at a white-faced German who was the same age as himself, he said, 'This is the man who fired two shots into an American prisoner-of-war'.

It was recorded in the newspapers the next day that ex-Private Georg Fleps instinctively shrank back as if the outstretched hand might strike him.

Samuel Dobyns followed. His testimony was close to Lary's. A German had fired a pistol. They had broken ranks. 'At least two machine guns opened up and we all hit the dirt. I was shot four times and there were eight to ten holes in my jacket. I saw three or four Germans shoot wounded men who were crying for help. I thought I was the only one left alive.'

Again the evidence was damning, but one of Everett's team, Lieutenant Wahler, did elicit from the ex-soldier during the cross-examination that the other prisoners *had broken ranks in response to the pistol shots but before the machine guns had opened up!*

But Lary's evidence, Dobyns' original evidence and that of Sergeant Ahrens which followed – 'When the Germans came over, they would say: "Is he breathing?" and would either shoot them or hit them with the butt of their guns' – blinded the panel to the significance of Dobyns' admission to Wahler. Was the whole bad business simply a tragic error, caused by one young trigger-happy soldier? But in the bitter anti-Nazi climate of the spring of 1946 very few Americans in Germany were prepared to ask that kind of question.

After his American witnesses Ellis called the Belgians. Madame Gregoire was particularly important to him because she could give a first-hand account of the massacre of the Legaye family and, being German-speaking, she could tell the court what the SS men had said to her at the time. She told her tale and then added that she and her two children had been the only ones spared by the SS murderers because of her knowledge of German. She admitted, however, that she, her children and other civilians were decently treated by the Germans for the next four days; in fact, they were later guided to a place of safety by the SS.

Under cross-examination by one of the defence's German lawyers, Dr Otto Leiling, Mme Gregoire admitted that she did not know whether or not other people were in the upper storeys of the house in which they had taken shelter that day. This left open the possibility that the SS had taken revenge for shots fired at them from up there. She also had to concede to Dr Leiling that heavy street fighting had been going on all day in Stavelot and 'there was shooting everywhere'.

The defence then suggested that the killings in the Amblève valley were in response to guerrilla activity on the part of the locals. But where were the guerrillas? Leiling did, however, score a minor victory when M. Jean Elias, the electrician from Trois Ponts, conceded that he had fought with the Americans in Maquis uniform. But that was all.

By now Everett knew that, although the American and Belgian witnesses were important to the prosecution's case, it really rested on the mass of sworn statements that the investigation team had gathered between December, 1945, and April, 1946. Now that he knew about them, Everett was struck by the fact that these 'statements', of which there were nearly a hundred, could be divided into two groups. One group was decidedly vague about the criminal acts allegedly committed; the other group was tremendously detailed, suspiciously so, in fact.

In addition, just before the case had opened, Everett had received reports from the SS prisoners that statements had been forced from them under duress. He reported this to the Judge Advocate of the Third Army but little came of it, save that a meeting was arranged between Ellis and Everett in which the former admitted that certain psychological 'stratagems' had been used to obtain statements, in particular 'mock trials'. But no action was taken.

Now, as the prosecution brought its case to a close, Ellis used the knowledge he had gained in the Judge Advocate's office to preclude any charges by the defence that underhand methods had been used to obtain confessions. Ellis told the court that, 'All the legitimate tricks, ruses and stratagems known to investigators were employed. Among other artifices used were stool-pigeons, witnesses who were not bonafide and ceremonies.' The black hood was produced which the prisoners had been forced to wear on certain occasions at Schwaebisch-Hall, but over and over again the prosecution denied any use of physical force.

The case of Arvid Freimuth was brought up. *He* wasn't at Dachau; he had hung himself in March, 1946, in his cell. All the same, the *unsigned* fragment of his statement was put forward by the prosecution as evidence. Perl, who had questioned Freimuth just before his suicide, admitted 'the possibility' that he had threatened to turn Freimuth over to the Belgians when he refused to co-operate. That was all.

Unfortunately for the defence, they got little further on this path, save for the admission from Perl and others who had examined the accused that the investigators had often drafted the statements *themselves* from their notes. These drafted statements had been set before the accused for signature. Naturally, according to the investigators, the prisoners had had the right to make textual changes. It was a minor advance for the defence. They had pried open several cracks in the prosecution's case. Yet the weight of evidence against the SS was massive. In a photograph taken of Colonel Ellis on the day the prosecution rested its case, he looks a man full of confidence, a man of clear conscience who is at ease with the world because he knows he has done a good job. The man in the photograph obviously didn't think there was a hope in hell for the prisoners. Let the 'Georgia Cracker' Everett try any way he liked, but at this stage of the game what could *he* pull out of the hat?

TWO

Everett knew he had to play for time. He had to find new evidence at Dachau and in Belgium. Therefore he opened his defence with an attack on the court itself. It was the same sort of attack used by most defending lawyers in war crimes trials. Everett challenged the court's jurisdiction. He declared that there could not have been any common ground for the murders, 'because these actions occurred during the most desperate combat situation of the war'. How could men involved in such a situation be tried by a court of law?

Colonel Rosenfeld did not let him get away with it. He called Everett to order and told him sternly that this was a duly constituted court of law, approved by the US authorities, and had a perfect right to try the defendants, as similiar courts had been trying other 'war criminals' since the previous summer.

Everett accepted the rebuke. He had been expecting it. Now he turned to the statements made at Schwaebisch-Hall and submitted they should be ruled inadmissible as evidence. Most of them, he contended, had been forced out of the SS men by threats and physical violence. Thereupon, he started to produce some of the *prosecution's* former witnesses, who had now been gained for the defence. One of them, Benno Agatha, testified that he had been forced to incriminate his former officers because 'I was told my parents were in Poland and the Poles would *take care* of them if I didn't co-operate.'

Marcel Boltz, another prosecution witness, from Alsace in France, said that a US officer had offered him safe conduct to his native country if he would testify against his commanding officer. He denied his former statement in which he had said, 'It was common knowledge' that Jochen Peiper had ordered the murders at the Baugnez cross-roads. He admitted he had made it without any knowledge of the matter.

Ellis challenged Everett. He reiterated his denial that duress had been used to obtain the statements, adding, with a queer kind of logic, that, even if they had, the statements would still retain their legal validity.

Here the court withdrew for twenty minutes to discuss whether the statements should be withdrawn or not. When it returned Colonel Rosenfeld, who now seemed openly against Everett, expressed the will of the bench. Without any explanation he stated that the defence's motion to withdraw the statements was denied.

On 20 June, after the trial had been running for nearly six weeks, Everett produced his star witness, Lieutenant-Colonel Hal McCown of the US Army. Peiper's former prisoner at La Gleize had been found working as an instructor at the Fort Benning School of Infantry. He made a good impression on most members of the panel save one, as we shall see later. Wavy-haired, clean-cut and with a boyish face, he had served as a regular officer since 1940. He had entered combat as an infantry officer in June, 1944 in Normandy and had served till the end of the war. Now he was undertaking something that needed as much courage as combat. Although he must have realized the danger to his own career in the Regular Army that might result from testifying on behalf of a 'war criminal', McCown went into the witness box to speak of his experiences during those four days in La Gleize. He made no secret of his admiration for Peiper. In his report written after his escape, McCown wrote of Peiper, 'I have met few men who impressed me in as short a space of time as did this German officer.'

Speaking in a soft southern accent, McCown described his imprisonment, testifying that the American prisoners, one hundred and thirty-five of them, mostly from his own regiment, had been well treated. He, personally, had observed only two minor infractions of the Geneva rules.

In his opening statement, Ellis had maintained that 'one hundred and seventy-five to three hundred and eleven' American prisoners and 'at least' three Belgians had been murdered by Peiper's men at La Gleize. Now McCown, an American who was there, was saying that there had been only one hundred and thirty-five American POWs with him in the cellar and they had been not harmed in any way! Immediately the defence had finished with their star witness, Captain Dwinnell of Ellis's staff sprang into action.

'Did you learn of any infractions of the Geneva rules?' he asked.

'I believe the two that I have mentioned (theft and poor food) are infractions of the Geneva rules,' McCown replied, 'but inasmuch as we are guilty of the same, I found no . . .'

'If the court pleases,' Dwinnell cut him off sharply, 'I object to that part of the answer.'

Again Rosenfeld sided with the prosecution. He ruled, 'The objection is sustained and that portion in the witness's statement as regards the actions of Americans will be stricken from the record and disregarded by the court.'

All that day the prosecution worked on McCown, but he still stuck to his testimony that Peiper had treated him and his fellow prisoners well and there had, in his opinion, been no shootings of American GIs in Peiper's hands.

If we are to believe the statement of ex-Private Zwigart, who had been Peiper's VW-jeep driver during the attack, Ellis went so far as to have one of the prosecution team visit him in his cell that evening. The American wanted Zwigart to testify that McCown had actually *guided* the escaping Germans through US lines that night and as a reward, McCown had been allowed to escape. According to the ex-driver's statement, when he refused to comply he was first beaten up and then promised that the charges against him (he was accused of murder) would be reduced. Again Zwigart refused and in the end the man from the prosecution gave up.

Though McCown had not wavered and had virtually destroyed one of the prosecution's major charges (the murder of several hundred Americans at La Gleize) by his testimony, the long conversation he admitted having with Peiper in the cellar weakened his statement. In the poisoned atmosphere of the Dachau court in 1946, there seemed something unwholesome about this lengthy talk between an American major and a German *Obersturmbannführer*. Besides, there is in every army an unwritten code which states that one rallies to the cause when there is trouble; there must be no breaking of the ranks. Now, here was an American soldier helping the former enemy in a case brought by the US Army!

Three years later Colonel Rosenfeld became highly emotional when he was forced to speak about McCown's testimony. 'I did not like McCown's testimony. That wasn't a question of a lawyer sitting on a bench evaluating this testimony. That was a question of one soldier who had been in combat evaluating another soldier who had been in combat. I just didn't like the manner in which he took the stand. I didn't like his manner on the stand and all the other members of the court agreed with me unanimously. I don't know whether McCown was telling the truth or not. I am glad to say this for the record, after three and a half years, I personally doubt the veracity of his testimony.

'Now, McCown and Peiper were entirely too friendly those nights they spent together. Peiper, with 600 (sic) of his men, was able to escape the trap when he was completely surrounded, and when he escaped McCown went with him; and then McCown simply said – and I think I am almost stating the exact words he said – it is in the record that, when they got to a certain stage in their march out of La Gleize, McCown simply walked off and Peiper went off in another direction with his 600 men.

'*I have no faith, and I am glad to say at this time, I didn't have one bit of faith in the testimony as given by the then Major McCown.*'

So much for Everett's star witness!*

Now Everett put Peiper, clearly the central figure in the case, in the dock. With his carefully groomed hair and soldierly bearing he scarcely looked like a beaten enemy. His attitude clearly expressed his disdain for the court. Let others grovel to the *Amis*, as he had seen some of his ex-comrades do during the trial. He would not.

Testifying on his own behalf in a faintly nasal baritone, he gave his story with little prompting. He told how he had been kept in a dark cell for five weeks in solitary confinement before he had been questioned by Lieutenant Perl. Obviously he was in a depressed psychological condition then. Perl had worked on him with a mixture of flattery and threats, indicating that he hadn't got a chance. What remained of his life could have only one purpose – to minimize the suffering of his comrades by assuming personal responsibility for the murders committed by his men.

Thereafter, having been confronted by several officers and men who accused him of having ordered the killings, he began to sign the statements. Totally demoralized, not by his own guilt, but by the complete breakdown of morale in his once proud *Kampfgruppe*, he had been prepared to sign *anything* that Perl wanted. In essence, he was innocent *personally*. But as a good commander he was responsible for the actions of his men, although he had not given any orders to commit atrocities.

Ellis naturally went to work on Peiper, the man to whom he had once said, 'I admire you', with a will. He knew he had to break him. Time and time again on that June day, Ellis tried to rattle him, but almost arrogantly Peiper stuck to his story. There were even moments, in that long cross-examination, of bitter humour. Dealing with alleged murders of Belgian civilians at Büllingen, Ellis asked Peiper, 'Did you

* Happily McCown survived to retire as a general in the US Army.

see an 80-year-old woman firing at you from the windows there in Büllingen?'

'In those short moments I had no occasion to determine the age of the person firing,' Peiper replied sardonically.

Ellis persisted: 'Did you see a one-year-old baby firing at you from the window in Büllingen?'

Peiper allowed himself a cold smile. 'No, not even in Russia did I see any one-year-old babies firing.'

Peiper was then allowed to make a personal statement in which he told the court about his first meeting with Ellis. Ellis, highly embarrassed, admitted that he *had* told Peiper how much he admired him and that he, Peiper, was sacrificing himself for a bunch of criminals. Ellis asked for Peiper's statement to be removed from the record, but this time Colonel Rosenfeld overruled him. The statement would remain, but he added that now very familiar qualification of his that the court would attach to the statement 'the value it deems necessary'.

Peiper thus was able to embarrass Ellis and win the duel of wits with him during the cross-examination; that was all. The case was still going very strongly against the accused.

During the ten-day recess in the trial, after the prosecution had finished its case, Everett sent one of his team, Major Miles Rulien, to retrace the *Kampfgruppe*'s route through Belgium. At the village of Büllingen, where Peiper had looted the gasoline, he discovered that one of the allegations made against the SS was untrue. There, according to the prosecution, an SS man had cold-bloodedly shot a Belgian woman through the head while she sat in a chair. The dead woman's husband, however, swore a statement that she had been killed by an exploding shell – *an American one*! It was a pity that Major Rulien had not gone a couple of streets further in the village. There he would have found 15-year-old Pfeiffer, who could have told him a great deal about what had happened at the crossroads; after all he had been there with Madame Bodarwé and Le Joly.

In La Gleize, too, he found someone who would testify for the defence. In his damaged house next to the school used by Peiper as his HQ, the village priest, Monsieur Blokiau, told the American that the charges against the Germans were untrue. Blokiau, no friend of a nation which had invaded his country twice in his lifetime, said there had been no slaughter of American POWs in his village. He had ventured out every day during the battle for La Gleize and the only dead American he had seen had been in the turret of a knocked-out Sherman tank. Gustav Sprenger was lying, too, when he had sworn he and his comrades had shot American prisoners lined up against a church wall. There wasn't such a wall and on the afternoon in question, Blokiau had walked round the church himself to inspect its damaged roof and had not seen a single dead American.

Several hundred murdered Americans would have been difficult to hide in such a small village. Other citizens testified that they would have known if any Americans had been murdered. Alfred Kreuz swore he saw no dead Americans during the course of the whole battle. Maria Gregoire said the same. In the village church where she sheltered, she saw Germans tending both their own and American wounded. The only American to die was one wounded in both legs. Armand Baltus, who lived close to the church, testified that no Americans were murdered at the cemetery wall. If there had been, he would have known, for he lived 'right there'.

Ellis took up the challenge again. He questioned Perl about his first meeting with Peiper. Had he really told Peiper he hadn't a chance because he had murdered the sons of a business tycoon and a senator at Malmédy? Perl denied it. Thon was asked whether he had beaten prisoners? Again a denial.

Ellis then turned his attention to the murder of the many Americans in La Gleize. He produced two statements from American soldiers back in the States who had apparently seen those elusive corpses. But these 'eyewitnesses' had seen over two hundred dead Americans in La Gleize on 22 December, 1944, *two days before Peiper had evacuated the place*! A cursory reading of their statements would have indicated that they were close copies of the finding and examination of the bodies at Baugnez. Obviously they had been faked. But, although Colonel Rosenfeld ruled that certain 'conclusions and assumptions' they contained should be disregarded, they were accepted as evidence.

Cynically, the defence noted that the prosecution was now contending La Gleize was not in Peiper's hands on 22 December, which contradicted not only historical fact but much of the prosecution's own previous evidence!

On Tuesday 9 July, 1946, the prosecution summarized the evidence against the prisoners. Captain Schumacher, taking over from Ellis, gave a final account of the events on that December day and ended in tones of high emotion: 'Today in America the survivors of these massacres, the mothers, fathers, sweethearts, wives and children of these comrades of ours who so needlessly fell, not on the field of battle, but from the tender mercies of the SS, are awaiting your findings. From their deaths there comes a clear understanding to our former enemies that they cannot wage warfare in a merciless and ruthless manner. They must learn that the end does not justify the means. It must be brought home to the German people that the principle of extermination which guided them in their last battle will not create for them a new and better world but will only bring disaster to their homeland and to themselves. Let their punishment be adequate for their crimes.'

On Wednesday, 10 July, the various defence lawyers summed up their case, with Everett making the final speech. He suggested to the panel that a fair and dispassionate judgement in the Malmédy case would assist the rise of a new 'democratic nationalism' in Germany and concluded with a quote from Tom Paine, that apostle of democracy: 'He that would make his own liberty secure must guard even his enemy from oppression, for if he violates this duty he establishes a precedent which will reach himself.'

It was recorded that ex-General Fritz Kraemer, who had once begged Peiper to reach that bridge at Huy with just one Tiger, wept openly. It was all over.

One of the greatest problems facing any trainer of soldiers in the West is to make the average soldier want to *kill*! Even when he trained, having run the whole range of brutalization to which the army usually subjects its men to make them kill in combat (and in the Second World War, let it be remembered, there was one British trainer who made his soldiers practise their bayonet skills in an abattoir, drenching them in buckets of animal blood as they ran at the dummies), they still will not kill.

As Brigadier S. L. A. Marshall, the American doyen of modern combat history, discovered to his surprise, when he interviewed infantrymen fresh from combat in France or the Pacific, even in 'highly motivated units' and when hard-pressed, no more than a quarter of all 'fighting soldiers' would use their weapons against the enemy. In *Men Against Fire* Marshall concluded that an army cannot 'unmake' Western man. 'It must reckon with the fact that he comes from a civilization in which aggression, connected with the taking of life, is prohibited and unacceptable. The teachings and ideals of that civilization are against killing, against taking advantage. The fear of aggression has been expressed to him so strongly and absorbed by him so deeply and pervadingly – practically with his mother's milk – that it is part of the normal man's emotional make-up. This is his greatest handicap when he enters combat. *It stays his trigger-finger even though he is hardly conscious that it is a restraint upon him.*' (author's italics).

It is the officers, normally, who make the soldier fight, and kill. Yet steadily over the last couple of centuries, officers in Western armies have withdrawn themselves from the nasty business of killing on the battlefield. In the days of individual combat, the knight (the officer of the time) was the most heavily armoured and weaponed man on the field. But since war was industrialized with the introduction of the hand-gun, the officer's withdrawal from the actual business of killing has been symbolized by the weapons he carries: a kind of small pike, a sword, and in our own time a pistol, usually kept holstered. In the First World War it was not unusual for an officer to go over the top armed solely with a cane or ashplant. Pictures taken of Peiper during the Ardennes offensive, for example, show him to be without even a pistol. Even the officer had to distance himself, symbolically at least, from the infliction of death. There is no reason to believe that the average German soldier or officer was any different from his British or American counterpart. Just as the Allied soldier had his 'mum' or 'schoolmarm' telling him he must not inflict pain or fight with others – it was 'naughty' – the German boy had his '*Mutti*' or '*Fraulein*' indoctrinating him with exactly the same message. Yet in the case of *Kampfgruppe* Peiper, we apparently have some 5,000 German soldiers murdering 1,000 prisoners and civilians in cold blood. Even in a totally criminal society, as might be found in a top security prison, this would be an incredibly high number of murderers. Indeed, when soldiers of the Royal Warwickshire Regiment reported after their repatriation during the war that elements of their battalion had been massacred by the SS at the little village of Wormhout in Northern France in 1940, it took them at least two years to convince British Army authorities that the massacre had really taken place. Although the famous Colonel Scotland, the scourge of the German war criminal, took up the case, nothing ever came of it. In the end the British authorities were convinced that other British troops had fired on the SS escort to the Warwick prisoners and this had been the cause of the outrage. For the British there would be no 'Malmédy' nor 'Aurich' trial in which Peiper's former comrade-in-arms, General Kurt Meyer of the 12th SS Division, the *Hitlerjugend*, was accused of murdering Canadian prisoners in Normandy.

Apparently those who ruled Britain in the mid-forties were realists who knew that unfortunate things happen on the battlefield and that they are never quite as they were reported by the shocked survivors of such incidents.

Later, after it was all over at Dachau, Colonel Everett had a few drinks with the president of the court, General Josiah Dalbey. If we are to believe Everett, Dalbey told him that Peiper and his men should never have been tried. Dalbey, who had been an Assistant Divisional Commander, knew that American soldiers had been guilty of similar offences, which was, of course, true. An officer and a sergeant in the US 45th Infantry, for example, cold-bloodedly shot down some forty-odd German prisoners in separate incidents. The killings were reported to General Patton (they had been witnessed by a British correspondent who later informed Captain Liddell Hart), who ordered the matter hushed up. Fortunately for Patton, the officer concerned was killed in combat. One year later another of Patton's armoured divisions was involved in the massacre of German prisoners not far from Malmédy. The matter was again hushed up. And we have the statement of the American engineer who witnessed the enraged American infantrymen leading off prisoners from Peiper's command to be shot outside Trois Ponts.

These things happen, *on both sides*. But they are rarely the way they are later reported by the survivors. How could they be? At the time those involved are usually in a highly emotional state, a heady mixture of fear, anger, and high tension. So what did happen at the Baugnez crossroads on that December day in 1944?

After the foundation of the Federal Republic of Germany in 1949, the apologists of the SS in Germany presumably felt it safe to begin discussing the Malmédy case – 'the law of the victor', as some of them pointedly called it. They maintained that the killings had been due to a misunderstanding. After the first group of Peiper's men had shot up the Battery B convoy, went the argument, they had disarmed the Americans and left them standing there to be picked up by the rear elements of the *Kampfgruppe*. But the US artillerymen, green as they were, had not been as tame as the SS had supposed. They had picked up their discarded weapons, and when the next group of Germans arrived, they had put up a fight and had been shot down. As evidence of this, the German apologists produced one lone NCO, a sergeant who had been wounded at the same crossroads half an hour *after* the Americans were killed. In other words, it had been a fair fight.

It is hardly a plausible case. The crossroads and the road leading to Baugnez from Büllingen and on to Ligneuville were under constant artillery fire from American guns on the heights to the right of the road. The sergeant could well have been a victim of that fire, as were a score of Belgian civilians.

If the artillerymen had downed their weapons the first time because they couldn't fight tanks with rifles and machine guns, why should they attempt to do so the second time? And, indeed, when young Pfeiffer crept out to inspect the bodies a quarter of an hour after the firing ceased, he found the bodies unarmed. As did Jose Velz, an adventurous fourteen-year old baker's apprentice, who examined the dead on the following Monday afternoon. Henri Le Joly is the one witness who finally destroys the SS apologists' case, for he maintains there was no break in the German presence at the crossroads. The Americans were under German guard all the time. According to Le Joly, the Americans had no chance of rearming themselves and putting up a fight. It was his impression too that they weren't particularly anxious to do so either.

Yet there are serious doubts about the official American presentation of the events at the crossroads that day. Did the unknown senior officer, presumed to be Major Werner Poetschke, actually give an order to kill the prisoners to the commander of the engineers, who then passed it on to one of his subordinate officers, who, in turn, gave it to Sergeant Siptrott, as the survivors assumed had happened?

Poetschke is dead. Siptrott, a laconic, broken man when interviewed by the author, was not speaking. Clotten denied the charge. Everything rests, and rested, on the testimony of Private Georg Fleps, the 'booty German' from Roumania.

One wonders, too, how the Americans, who gave no evidence that they spoke German, could follow what their enemies were saying. Ford, the military policeman, mentions the Germans going from American to American asking, 'Is he breathing?' after the 'massacre'. Others recorded other incidents spoken in German. How did they know, unless they spoke the language themselves?

And, finally, was it an order that started the shooting? Or was it Fleps firing the pistol at the Americans which started the 'stampede'? We have Dobyns' testimony to support this theory. After all, the woods were nearby and there were only two tanks crewed by ten men actually guarding the estimated one hundred and fifty prisoners. Doesn't the fact that some forty-four men, *nearly one in three*, managed to escape initially, seem to indicate that it was not a systematic massacre, but a sudden panicky attempt by a couple of tank crews to stop their prisoners getting away?

Although at the trial Colonel Ellis tried to prove that Dietrich, following Hitler's directive, deliberately instructed his men to massacre whatever prisoners they took and any civilians they thought suspicious, he could find no written evidence to back up his claim. The Sixth's war diaries were never found, in which such directives would have been recorded (one source states they were destroyed in May, 1945). At Nuremberg, during the trial, Field-Marshal von Rundstedt and Colonel-General Jodl both denied that such an order had been given. Probably, what Dietrich had meant when he had ordered the 'usual treatment' for prisoners was to send them to the rear; and, after all, the Sixth did take seven thousand prisoners and not murder one of them. It is, therefore, strange that all the alleged atrocities committed in the Ardennes were limited to one unit of some five thousand men out of three whole armies, numbering some half a million soldiers.

In other words, the *Leibstandarte* did not cross the Belgian border on the evening of 16 December, 1944, with the express intention of massacring every American soldier captured. If nothing else prevented them doing so, the knowledge, at least among their officers, that the war was already lost and they could well be called to account for any crimes committed, certainly would have stopped them. The *Leibstandarte* crossed the border that day intent on driving to the Meuse, a military objective. Time was of the essence and they wouldn't waste it on POWs. But that didn't mean they would massacre them to rid themselves of the burden, as has been suggested by one historian.

Of the two Belgian eye-witnesses who were present all the time at the crossroads before the Café Bodarwé was set ablaze and Madame Bodarwé disappeared for good, only Henri Le Joly survived to give his account.

Le Joly, as we have already noted, was pro-German (indeed at the time of the trial he was serving a prison sentence in Verviers, accused by the Belgians of spying for the Germans) and had seen just how overwrought the young SS men were that day. Before he had gone over to the Café from his farmhouse opposite, a tank had pulled up just in front of him. One of the two boys in the turret pulled out a pistol and fired at him. Le Joly protested that he was German himself. The boy didn't seem to hear. He fired again, and missed. Le Joly didn't attempt any further explanation. He fled into the house and went down to the cellar. To his surprise he found an elderly German refugee, an ex-First World War soldier from Cologne, and an unknown Belgian boy of eighteen, sheltering there. A few moments later there was a tremendous roar and the cellar shook as a shell from the tank wrecked the kitchen above.

'Why are they shooting at us?' the man from Cologne demanded. 'We're German, too! Tell them we're German and they're still in Germany.'

Foolishly Le Joly decided to do so. He clambered up the stairs and waded through the smoking rubble of his kitchen. A sergeant was standing in the turret of the tank. Wordlessly he crooked a finger at Le Joly. The latter shook his head and beckoned the German.

Followed by the two SS men, the sergeant came cautiously down the muddy track to Le Joly's one-storey stone farmhouse.

'Why are you shooting at us?' Le Joly demanded. 'We're as German as you. My father fought in the Great War and my grandfather in the War of '70.'

By now the old man from Cologne had also emerged from the cellar. 'That's right,' he said hotly. 'I'm German, too. I fought in the Great War as well.' He held out his paybook with the names of the battles in which he had fought inscribed in it. The NCO calmed down. 'We saw somebody running across the fields to your house,' he explained. 'We thought it was an *Ami* or a partisan.' Le Joly presumed he was referring to the strange youth in the cellar.

The two younger Germans started making threatening gestures. One of them shouted, 'I'll take you into that field and shoot you!'

'But I'm as German as you,' Le Joly persisted.

'You're all spies and traitors at the border,' the SS man yelled back.

The NCO, realizing that the situation was getting out of hand, cried, 'Get back into the cellar! I can't restrain them much longer!'

Le Joly didn't need to be told twice.

This was the mood of some of the SS men, as Le Joly and Madame Bodarwé watched the prisoners at the crossroads a little later. The Americans didn't seem to be very concerned, but certainly Le Joly was, after his recent experience, and now he heard some of the Germans talking angrily about the alleged killing of one of their comrades by three American prisoners who had escaped from Büllingen.

'There was tension in the air,' he said years later. (One might ask why Le Joly ventured out again, but in that remote area little happens. Anything new, even if it was potentially dangerous, was of interest. Besides, there were officers present now to control the excitable young SS men.)

For a while they watched the tanks rolling by in much the same way as they had watched the pre-war traffic coming back after a day's racing at the nearby Francochamps Race Track. Then there was a lull and only two tanks and a handful of SS infantry were left. Suddenly a single shot rang out. Le Joly didn't see the man who fired it, but presumably it was Fleps. Le Joly saw the Americans break ranks. He heard a cry in German, but he can no longer remember the precise words. It might have been, '*Schlagt die tot, die Hunde!*' ('kill them, the dogs'.) At all events it was then that the machine guns began firing. The Americans who hadn't already scattered began to fall, dead or wounded. Le Joly counted twenty-five to thirty of them (Josef Veltz, the baker's boy, confirms this figure). Now as the SS started to spread out, Le Joly fled to his farm and Madame Bodarwé to her Café, never to be seen again.

This, then, is the account of what happened at the crossroads by a man who was pro-German and who suffered because of it (he spent three years in prison). There was no reason for him to support the American thesis of a massacre at the crossroads. It is supported by Samuel Dobyns' testimony, too. So we have, in the end, not a premediated massacre, but an expression of individual violence which ended in tragedy for all concerned, not only for the victims shot that day, but for nearly three score other men, some guilty, some innocent. They would all have to live with the memory of that day until age itself – or, in one case, until a similar act of violence – overtook them.

On 15 July, 1946, the accused were marched into a packed courtroom. The cameramen and journalists were back. Today the sentences would be passed.

General Dalbey deepened the already depressed atmosphere by beginning with the answer to the prisoners' request to be shot instead of hanged if found guilty of murder. Those sentenced, he announced, would be hanged. Grimly, he warned the spectators to be silent during sentencing. He wanted no displays of emotion. Then he called the first defendant who had given the trial its official title, US v Bersin: 'Valentin Bersin.'

Bersin rose, marched smartly across the court and stood rigidly to attention in front of the general. Everett did the same and stood at his side, as he would at the sides of all the rest.

'Valentin Bersin,' Dalbey read, 'the Court in close session, at least two thirds of its members present at the time when the vote was taken concurring, sentences you to death by hanging at such a time and place as higher authority may direct.'

One by one the defendants were brought before the general – on average he passed a sentence every two minutes – to hear their fate. Private Georg Fleps, who had fired the first shot – death by hanging. Knittel, whose reconnaissance battalion had carried out that fatal mission in the Amblève valley – death by hanging.

On and on it went – forty-three death sentences, twenty-two sentences of life imprisonment; two sentenced to twenty years, one to fifteen and five to ten years; seventy-three sentences in all. Sepp Dietrich, the oldest of the accused, received life, as did the youngest, Fritz Gebaur, who had been sixteen years old at the time.

All the time Everett stared rigidly ahead, his eyes fixed on some distant horizon known only to himself. The next day he wrote to his wife of his heart being 'crushed' by the sentences and his head, 'whirling, splitting and hammered'.

'*Schuldig, schuldig. Tod durch Erhängen; Tod durch Erhängen*', over and over again the interpreter translated the General's words, the heavy atmosphere broken only by the stiffled sob of one of the accused's relatives and the stamp of their boots as the prisoners marched back and forth.

Now it was Peiper's turn. A few days before he had written what he believed would be his last letter to Everett. His men, he had written, 'are the products of total war, grown up in the streets of scattered towns without any education. The only thing (they) knew was to handle weapons for the Reich. They were young people with a hot heart and the desire to win or die according to the word: right or wrong – my country. When seeing today the defendants in the dock, don't believe them to be the old combatgroup Peiper. All my old friends and comrades have gone before. The real outfit is waiting for me in Valhalla.'

But this morning all explanations, justifications, indeed all emotion had vanished. His face was pale but expressionless as General Dalbey read out the verdict and then the sentence.

Softly the interpreter translated the words into German: '*Tod durch Erhängen*'.

But Peiper did not need his services. He had understood already. Quite clearly, in a voice audible to everyone in the court, he said, '*Danke*'. Then he turned smartly and strode back to his place.

By the time people in America were opening their papers and sipping their first cup of coffee, it was all over. The 'Malmédy Massacre Trial' was finished. In the late editions of that day, the papers would write of the trial: 'Because the conscience of humanity has not quite been stilled ... the world reaches out for a concept of international law' and 'The

Nazi philosophy of ruthlessness . . . and the policy of frightfulness as an end in itself stood also at the bar of judgment and were found guilty.'

Back in Dachau a triumphant Colonel Ellis was telling the noisy journalists eager for a story, 'They (the SS) showed no more emotion than if they had been eating a meal. They marched in, snapped to attention, listened to their sentence and then, doing an about-face, marched off.'

Colonel Everett could not be found.

THREE

In that autumn of 1946 in Germany there was precious little justice, honour or courage to be found. *Zivilcourage*, as the Germans call the capacity to stand up and say one's piece without fear, was a dead virtue. The country was beginning to starve.

As Field-Marshal Montgomery told his listeners in a speech in Britain, the average German was receiving fewer calories daily than the inmates of Bergen-Belsen concentration camp had received in the last year of the war (probably most of his listeners thought that that was all they deserved). Ten marks bought an American cigarette and twenty such cigarettes could buy the sexual favours of a 'frowlein', for the most part starving amateurs who thronged the pavements around the US Army PXs in the larger south German cities. From Dusseldorf there came reliable reports of cannibalism and there were food riots in nearby Cologne which were hushed up by the British occupation authorities.

A few voices were raised in protest at the sentences imposed on the SS at Dachau. Dr Wurm, a prominent Protestant churchman, and Cardinal Frings, a close friend of the rising German politician Konrad Adenauer, were among those few. But for the most part, the struggle for survival was a full enough occupation for the Germans. Besides, were not the sentenced killers members of the SS, they asked. Didn't they deserve what they got after what they had done in the concentration camps? The SS had become the alibi for a whole nation.

'Who wouldn't have despaired for Germany in those days?' Peiper wrote years later. 'Now *we* were the flotsam of the Second World War.'

That autumn the Malmédy men were transferred to Landsberg Prison, where in 1924 Hitler had dictated *Mein Kampf* to Hess, while the two of them were serving a prison sentence after the abortive Munich putsch. Here they were housed on the ground floor, reserved, according to American prison usage, for men sentenced to death. They were fitted out with red jackets (*Rotjacken*) which identified them as members of the 'death house'. But they were not alone in the 'death house'. Another three hundred *Rotjacken* were imprisoned there, awaiting execution, which was always signalled by a guard entering a man's cell and demanding, 'Bible, blankets and pictures'. Then, after a few prayers mumbled by the prison chaplain and a short walk to the gallows erected in the courtyard, it was all over. Another war criminal was dead.

For the first time Frau Peiper and her small children were allowed to visit the condemned man. Frau Peiper kept the information that soon their father was to die carefully from the children. Many years later Elke Peiper said, 'We always thought our father was a prisoner-of-war of the Americans, just like most other children's fathers at that time. A couple of times a year our mother would take us to Landsberg to visit Father. We were happy to see him, of course, but we were more fascinated by the guards everywhere and the strange red jackets that many of the prisoners wore.'

So the 'red jackets' waited for the word from the American Commander of the US Zone of Occupation, General Clay. Would he confirm the sentence of death passed on them at Dachau?

But no word came. For three years in most cases and for *four years and seven months* in Peiper's case, the forty-three men waited for his decision. As Peiper wrote in 1952, 'Only those who have lost their freedom can understand just how long a day is, what a nightmare it is not to know what is going to happen for four years and seven months, alone in a space of twenty-three square centimetres in which one's whole being lives on tip-toes.'

Slowly the outside world began to forget about them. 'Nothing reminded us of life but our eternally rumbling stomachs and the song of the birds at dawn and dusk. Oh, you birds, was there ever a prisoner who did not gain new hope from your song?'

Unknown to Peiper and the rest, there was a faint glimmer of hope on the horizon. Everett, now released from the Army, was back in his practice in Georgia; filled with a sense of bitterness because he believed a great injustice had been done at Dachau, he fought desperately to obtain a review of the trial. Over the months and the years, with plenty of time at last to present a properly organized and detailed case, Everett tackled the US authorities, going right to the top at the

Pentagon to gain first a stay of execution and if possible a new trial. In the end it was to take him ten years. It cost him his health and, according to one American writer, forty thousand dollars of his own money, before he finally achieved his purpose.

In 1947 he had his first small success. He managed to obtain a stay of execution. One year later, however, on 20 March, 1948, General Clay confirmed the death sentence on twelve of the accused, including Peiper. The death sentences on the others were reduced to life imprisonment. One month later thirteen of the Malmédy men, including four originally sentenced to death, were released for good. On 20 May that year General Clay ordered that the twelve whose death sentences he had confirmed should be executed at once. But Clay was twenty-four hours too late. Washington had changed its mind.

On the evening of 19 May Secretary of the Army Mr Royall had wired US Army Headquarters in Heidelberg that there would be no executions and that all death sentences would be reviewed. The second battle to save Peiper and the rest had begun.

What was going to happen now had nothing to do with justice. The post-war honeymoon between the two new superpowers, the United States and Russia, was over. Now the two wartime allies, who had divided the world between them at the expense of two colonial empires and most of Central Europe, glared at each other over the zonal frontier in Germany, making warlike noises. Eisenhower, who had felt he could get on with Stalin and that America had nothing to fear from the USSR, had gone home. Clay, who succeeded him, now submitted a secret report to the Pentagon, predicting that Russia and the USA might soon be at war. In London Churchill was suggesting that, by threatening to drop the atom bomb, the Western Allies could blackmail the Russians into getting rid of Stalin. As for Stalin himself, he had about completed the process of gobbling up most of Central Europe and was now preparing to tackle West Germany.

Clear-thinking Americans were coming round to the realization that the starved, beaten Germans were the key to everything. The twentieth century was and would be the 'German century', as far as Western Europe was concerned. France and Italy, both plagued by internal differences and large communist parties, would not be the arbiters of the continent's fate; neither would Great Britain, busy shedding its Imperial burden in order to pay for the new Welfare State. The future wealth of the Middle East was given up so that the socialists could buy false teeth and specs for old ladies in Luton. If anyone could present a bulwark against the Russians, in accordance with the new Truman Doctrine of containment of the 'Red Threat', it would be the Germans.

But would the economic and political titbits offered the West Germans be enough? Already they had been given the currency reform, which ended the black market, and the three zones were being organized into one political unit, Trizonia. Would this suffice, however, to induce the West Germans to re-arm when the time came? After all, many members of the former *Wehrmacht* still languished in Allied POW camps and there was wide-spread anti-militarism in the West. '*Ohne mich*' (without me) was the slogan of the time. Understandably so, when the old *Wehrmacht* had been so discredited by the Allied courts in 1946 and 1947. Thus it was against this kind of background that, in July, 1948, Secretary of the Army Royall sent a three-man commission to Germany to investigate the Malmédy trial and the cases of some one hundred other Germans sentenced to death or life-imprisonment by the Dachau court.

Under the presidency of Judge Simpson, the commission started the whole weary business once again, taking statements from all the Germans imprisoned in Landsberg, all the civilians who had been employed at Schwaebisch-Hall during the discredited interrogations, and those of the War Crimes Team still in Germany. It was at this time that most of the prisoners swore their affidavits on the nature of the treatment handed out to them during the interrogations.

In his sworn statement, Peiper detailed every stage of his interrogation from his first meeting with Mr Paul at Freising in August, 1945, until his 'confession' to Lieutenant Perl at Zuffenhausen the following November. He ended it with the words: 'An outsider cannot understand the background to the Malmédy case without a detailed study of the psychological framework. A purely formal review of the case will always remain a patchwork.' How true that was Peiper little realized. No one, including Peiper himself, would ever really know what happened at that crossroads!

The three judges Simpson, van Roden and Lawrence, all expressed concern at the 'tricks and ruses' employed by the investigators. Nevertheless they professed to be satisfied with the twelve death sentences, including Peiper's, which had been confirmed by General Clay. They thought, however, that if the defendants had been Americans, life imprisonment would have been a more suitable sentence and recommended that all death sentences should be commuted to life imprisonment.

They rejected Everett's claim that physical violence had been inflicted on the prisoners to get them to talk and rejected the evidence offered by others in Schwaebisch-Hall, orderlies, dentists etc, that there had been beatings. Although he signed the joint Simpson

Commission Report, as it was called, Judge van Roden was not totally satisfied. On his return to the USA he told journalists what he had told representatives of the European Press: 'In all of the 139 cases, with the exception of two, that we investigated, the Germans had been kicked in the testicles.' Now the fat was in the fire. The Simpson Report was unable to sweep the dirt under the carpet. Suddenly the fate of the twelve condemned men at Landsberg became a hot political issue, and there was one up-and-coming young American politician who was going to grab it with both hands.

By the end of 1948 there was a growing number of influential politicians demanding that something had to be done about 'Malmédy'. That October the influential *New York Times* stated 'that a decent respect for the opinion of others demands that no final action be taken . . . until a complete and satisfying explanation is given'.

In that same month the *Denver Post* wrote : 'When you think of the bodies of those kids, the fury of such postwar gentleness toward their executioners gets hot within you. Then you remember the chain reaction that is set off and how we took mighty few prisoners before the whole tale was told and your conclusions become bitterly confused.'

One year, almost to the day, after General Clay had made his first move in the Malmédy case the three-man Senate sub-committee met for the first time to look into allegations that the Dachau trial had been based on evidence gained under duress. Its chairman was Senator Baldwin, who was really too old at that time to be entrusted with such a job. He also had an unfortunate personal and *undeclared* interest in the case, since the former head of the early stages of the interrogation of the Malmédy men, ex-Captain Fanton, was now closely associated with the law firm of which Baldwin was a member.

Baldwin was assisted by a well-known, younger senator named Kefauver who never quite lived up to his early promise. He, too, had a personal interest in the case. He had practised law in the same firm as Raphael Schumacher, second in prominence to Ellis on the prosecution team. Kefauver had openly proclaimed that Schumacher was 'a friend of mine for whom I had the highest regard'. The third member was Senator Lester C. Hunt of Wyoming.

Given the composition of the inquiry and the personal inclinations of the first two members, it could be assumed that everything would have gone off smoothly with a result that would be favourable to the investigation and prosecution teams – save for one thing. When the inquiry met for the first time on Monday 18 April in Room 212 of the Senate Office Building, they were joined by an uninvited and unwished-for guest, who demanded not only to cross-examine those witnesses called by the inquiry but the right to summon witnesses of his own. *The junior senator from Wisconsin, Joe McCarthy, had appeared on the scene.*

FOUR

In the twentieth century it has seemed to be America's fate to over-react to unpleasant political events overseas. After the First World War America fled from the mess of the new Europe she had helped to create into two decades of isolationism and was only persuaded to come out of it by President Roosevelt's cunning policies. In our own time the defeat in Vietnam resulted in the Watergate scandal, the downfall of an American President and the emergence of a modified kind of new isolationism.

In the late 'forties and early 'fifties, seemingly frightened by the way that Europe was becoming ever more inclined to communism, and with the Cold War rapidly turning into the hot one of Korea, there were those in American political life who felt an hysterical, almost pathological, need to root out 'subversion' wherever it could be found in the United States. In every branch of political, economic, academic and artistic endeavour, Americans were called upon to kneel and kiss the rod of the various oaths of loyalty demanded from them, or face the consequences.

The man whose name was to become synonymous with that unhappy era of American history tried the technique he was later to perfect for the first time in the Malmédy inquiry. The ex-Marine Corps captain, who had been helped into office by his frequent references to his 'war wounds' (as a member of the Navy's legal department it is hardly likely that he ever heard a shot fired in anger), was probably attracted to the Malmédy hearing because he sensed 'an issue': a chance to get his name in the headlines, something he dearly loved all his short, hectic political life. Another consideration was that many of his voters in Wisconsin were of German-American stock and up to recently had been proud of it. Due to the fact that so many concerned with the investigation at Schwaebisch-Hall and the later trial were Jewish, there was also the appeal, unexpressed of course, to the many anti-Semites in the States. Whatever his motives, McCarthy now started to attend Senator Baldwin's committee and to perfect that technique – the smear, the threat, the half-truth, the often cited but rarely produced 'key witness' – that was to make him the most feared man in US politics in the 'fifties.

Of course McCarthy realized the dangers he was running by taking the German side. He had to avoid giving the impression that he wanted German war criminals mollycoddled, while at the same time he wanted to discredit the committee and US military justice in Occupied Germany. Playing on his own largely imaginary war record in the Pacific, he was in action within minutes of the inquiry opening, droning on in his humourless montone: 'Every member of the committee realizes the gruesomeness of the crime perpetrated over there. I think every member of our committee feels that when the guilty are found and properly tried, they should either be hung over whatever sentence happens to be meted out to them . . . (but) in all the unusual reports coming out of the European Theater, some of us were very much concerned in checking to see exactly what type of justice we are meting out in Germany.'

McCarthy had made his position clear. Now he prepared to 'lam into' the witnesses, as he bluntly expressed it.

Ex-Sergeant Ken Ahrens, one of the survivors, soon felt the full brunt of his rage. When he explained that the SS had laughed and joked as they walked the ranks of the fallen, shooting those who were still alive, McCarthy sprang to his feet and shouted that Ahrens' testimony was 'trying to inflame the public and the members of the committee' and was nothing more than an attempt to start a 'Roman holiday'. Ahrens, who by this time had his evidence off pat, was seen to turn pale under this attack and lose his air of confidence.

But Senator McCarthy reserved his full treatment for those who had done the investigating at Schwaebisch-Hall, in particular for Dr Perl, who unfortunately (for him) was very self-assured and long-winded. Once, while the meaning of the term 'heat of combat' was being discussed, Perl suggested innocently that McCarthy perhaps didn't know what the phrase meant. McCarthy exploded, 'I am under no misconception as to the meaning of what "in the heat of combat" is. You may be. I don't know whether you saw any combat or not. But don't tell me I don't know what the heat of combat is.'

Honour satisfied for the while, McCarthy let Perl ramble on in his long-winded way until he said that there had been no physical violence used at Schwaebisch-Hall to obtain confessions. That did it. Again McCarthy was on his feet, jaw stuck out angrily.

'I think you're lying!' he roared at Perl. 'You may be able to fool us. I have been told that you are very, very smart, but I am convinced you cannot fool *the lie detector*!'

This was the first mention of the famous lie detector which became such an important feature of the Malmédy hearing and of subsequent hearings in McCarthy's infamous career.

Next he turned his venom on the prosecution lawyers. He treated Baldwin's associate Fanton gently and dealt with Schumacher, Kefauver's friend, with some restraint; after all he was no fool and they were powerful senators. But the kid gloves were off when Colonel Ellis made his appearance. He would receive the full treatment. After Ellis had told the committee about the mock trials held at Schwaebisch-Hall to make the prisoners confess, McCarthy took a letter out of the bulging briefcase which he always kept close to his side, as if it contained some great treasure or precious secret, and began to read. The letter was from James Bailey, who had been the court recorder to the nine-man interrogation team. In it Bailey claimed that the evidence against the Germans had been obtained by 'starvation, brutality and threats of bodily harm'. Eventually he could stomach the treatment of the prisoners no longer and had asked for a transfer to another outfit. McCarthy let his words sink for a moment, staring hard at Ellis before accusing him of making a 'mockery of justice', of manufacturing evidence and using methods 'so brutal as to be repulsive'. And off he went on the rampage, detailing the smashed genitals which seemed to fascinate him, before allowing Ellis to continue.

Ellis described the use the investigators had made of blacked-out rooms, hooded figures posing as priests, lighted candles, swinging nooses, mock trials and the rest of the mumbo-jumbo that they had employed at Schwaebisch-Hall. But, he added, he had always thought the prisoners had known all the time they were attending mock trials because they had not been assigned a proper defence lawyer.

McCarthy looked at him aghast and then burst out, '*You can't mean that!*'

Obviously Ellis did. McCarthy drew more facts about his legal training out of Ellis and now, dominating the whole hearing, made the point that Ellis 'showed a complete lack' of knowledge of criminal procedure and that the US Army had been severely at fault for having assigned him to the case. This was McCarthy's first, if indirect, attack on the Army, which would bring him so many public triumphs later.

Returning to the mock trials, McCarthy asked Ellis, 'You believed it proper to use mock trials to gain confessions so long as you informed the court?'

Ellis answered that he did believe it 'perfectly proper', adding, 'But I was opposed to the use of beatings to obtain confessions.'

It was an unfortunate choice of words, for it gave his listeners the impression that there *had* been beatings after all.

And so it went on, with McCarthy relentlessly breaking down the prosecution team's case and making a mockery of the committee, in particular of the ageing Senator Baldwin.

At one point McCarthy demanded that all the judges who had tried the defendants at Dachau should be given lie-detector tests. He then made the same demand of Baldwin himself, who, McCarthy insinuated, had something to hide, which indeed he had, in the shape of ex-Major Fanton. Mercilessly McCarthy heckled Baldwin until finally he referred McCarthy's demand to the all-powerful Senate Armed Services Committee. Naturally they voted it down.

McCarthy had shot his bolt, but he had gained some valuable national publicity by his heckling of the witnesses and the committee; it would ensure he'd gain a few more votes in his home state the next time round. It was time for him to abandon the hearing. But then, and for the next six years of his tumultuous career, Senator Joseph McCarthy never just *left* a hearing; he staged what he and the Press were wont to call a 'disgusted walk-out'.

On Friday 20 May, 1949, he did just that. In the course of the morning's hearing he rose to claim that the Army was mollycoddling sadists and that the unfortunate Baldwin was trying to whitewash the Army's role in the Dachau trial. His words were salted with lurid references to men screaming under torture until they were only too eager to sign a confession. The torturers had used 'brutalities greater than any we have accused the Russians or Hitler's Germany of employing'.

He knew what was going on. He knew that Senator Baldwin had personal reasons for not wanting to discover the truth. Here McCarthy touched that famous bulging briefcase knowingly, as if its contents could reveal some tremendous secret. No, he would no longer be a party to 'this farce, this deliberate and clever attempt to whitewash the military . . . for which Baldwin was criminally responsible'. He was leaving *now*.

In the general uproar that followed one man had the presence of mind to follow the irate Senator from Wisconsin into the corridor outside. He was Richard Rovere, a clever youngish reporter, then working for *The New Yorker*. As he recalled years later, he asked McCarthy why he was so excited. By way of answer, McCarthy touched his briefcase and said, 'These documents will speak for themselves.' He lifted it to give Rovere some indication of the weight of the incriminating material it contained. 'When you've looked at a few of my documents,' he told Rovere, 'you'll agree with me that this is one of the most outrageous things this country has ever known.'

Thinking he had a scoop on his hands, Rovere asked to see these world-shaking documents.

McCarthy refused. 'You'll see them all right,' he said grimly. 'I'm not holding anything back. I'm through with this lousy investigation. I'm taking my case to the public.' And with that he was gone.

Senator McCarthy, of course, never did take his case to the public. No one ever learnt what tremendous secrets that bulging briefcase contained. But the Senator's intervention in the Malmédy case had its effect.

Secretary of the Army Royall now lost his nerve. McCarthy's 'disclosures' could be unfortunate for the Army. He ordered that no executions would be carried out in the case of the 'Malmédy men' imprisoned at Landsberg. Thus Jochen Peiper undoubtedly owed his life to the rabble-rousing Junior Senator from Wisconsin.

The months in Landsberg dragged into years. Outside things were changing in West Germany. The zones of occupation had been wound up. The Federal Republic had been created. The black market was dead. There was plenty of food in the stores again. Already the 'economic miracle' had begun. The Germans were driving cars again. German money in the form of the new 'hard D-Mark' was crossing the Atlantic to hire the services of American lawyers to fight the case of the 'Landsberg criminals' and lobby government agencies in their favour.

As 1950 gave way to 1951, the Malmédy sentences had been under review since the autumn and Everett, still fighting for his former clients, was optimistic. His optimism was not misplaced. On 30 January, 1951, the Commander-in-Chief of the US Seventh Army in Germany, General Thomas Handy, announced that the six Malmédy prisoners still under sentence of death would have their sentences commuted to life imprisonment. In rare good humour, Peiper wrote to Everett that day:

'We have received a great victory and, next to God, it is you (from) whom our blessings flow. In all the long and dark years you have been the beacon flame for the forlorn souls of the Malmédy boys, the voice and the conscience of the good America, and yours is the present success against all the well-known overwhelming odds. May, I, therefore, Colonel, express the everlasting gratitude of the red-jacket team as well as of all the families concerned.'

Jochen Peiper could take off that red jacket at last. That evening young Elke Peiper came home from school, schoolbag on her back, face flushed with the cold, to find her mother 'beside herself with excitement'.

'What's the matter, *Mutti*?' she asked.

'*Papi ist heute begnadigt worden*' (Daddy was pardoned today), her mother cried, eyes shining with excitement.

'Suddenly I realized for the first time that he would not be hanged after all,' the woman who was then a ten-year old schoolgirl remembers today, 'that one day somehow he would be coming home to us.'

PART V

The Old Man of Traves

Gatsby believed in the green light, the orgiastic future that year by year recedes before us. It eluded us then, but that's no matter – tomorrow we will run faster, stretch out our arms farther. . . . So we beat on, boats against the current, borne back ceaselessly into the past.

F. Scott Fitzgerald: The Great Gatsby

ONE

In June, 1951, the last seven redjackets were hanged at Landsberg. They included such mass-murderes as Otto Ohlendorf, Oswald Pohl and Captain Schmidt, the former adjutant at Buchenwald concentration camp. His speciality had been garrotting and hanging up his victims on meat hooks. Now he died on the gallows himself, crying, 'I die for Germany'.

Far away in Hanover some unrepentant Nazi placed a wreath on the local war memorial, bearing the words, 'For those murdered at Landsberg'.

Now those who represented Peiper's interest in the States felt the time had come to have him freed, even if only on parole. But they didn't get far. In Washington Senator Kefauver declared that as long as he had anything to say in the United States, he'd undertake that the 'German Colonel' was never released from prison.

That winter Peiper wrote a long essay from his cell, which was later included in a collection of wartime memoirs of the *Waffen SS*, edited by ex-General Hausser. It begins as if it were being written by a man twice his age. 'In his lonely cell sits a war criminal on a stool and dozes. On his door the sign says "life" and on the calendar the date is October, 1952. The stove sings, the spider is looking for new winter positions and autumn is shaking the cell windows with a rough hand.'

But the bitterness about his fate soon came through. 'Thirteen years now separate me from my wife, my birthday celebrated five times as a man sentenced to death and now before me this eighth Christmas in jail. Really a sunny youth I've spent! One wouldn't treat an animal that badly.'

He goes on in the same vein: 'The news which managed to penetrate our cells from outside was not exactly calculated to make the manner of our dying any easier. We learnt that we belonged to a criminal organization and that we had served an unjust state. The flood of memoirs from ex-generals and ex-diplomats revealed that their main activity (during the war) had been to bring down that state. One felt like Decius Muz who had landed in a manure heap!'

Looking back at the war years when he had fought so loyally for that 'unjust state', Peiper described how they now seemed to him like an 'Icarus journey through a sun-filled sky'. That was all over now, he told his unknown readers, but they should remember that the bodies of dead SS soldiers had formed a barricade in the East against the threat posed to the culture of the West by the Slav hordes.

'Don't forget,' he wrote, 'that it was in the ranks of the SS that the first "Europeans" died. . . . Today that European idea is the only one worth fighting for. Never have we been closer to the realization of this idea. Throttle the lie; strike slander in the face; help your neighbour and the war widow. Only if we can find our way back to the simple values . . . and make a virtue out of poverty can we get things moving again and erect those barriers necessary for the day when the deluge descends upon us.'

Peiper ended his homily with the following words: 'During the war our divisions (those of the SS) were regarded as particularly stable in times of crisis. In the jails of the world we have proved just how steadfast we are. Let us hope that one day our children will say we were not meaner than our fate and that even in our Diaspora we contributed to the idea of reconciliation and the European movement. *I salute all who have remained free in prison!'*

It was a moving piece of writing. Despite its acknowledgement of contemporary political issues, the Cold War and the European movement, it was really the product of a man who felt bitter at his fate but had become resigned to it. Peiper knew he would never serve thirty-five years in jail (though if he had known what was to be the fate of the last war criminal, Hess, he might not have been so sanguine). All the same he saw no hope of release for himself in the near future. The time was not yet ripe although there were strong factions in American political and public life who were still fighting hard to ensure that he was allowed to go free.

By 1954, seventeen further 'Malmédy men' had been released, having served their sentence allowing for the deduction for 'good time'. Now there were about thirty of them left in Landsberg, thirteen, including Peiper, serving what was virtually a life sentence. In that year the US Senate's Watkins Committee began to investigate the conduct of

Senator McCarthy, who had saved Peiper's life. His latest attacks on the US Army, which had begun with the Malmédy hearing, had gone too far.

The one-time Supreme Commander, who had ordered the initial inquiry into what had happened at the crossroads at Baugnez and was now President of the United States, was stung into supporting the Army at last. McCarthy had accused General Zwicker of being 'unfit to wear' US uniform. (He had commanded a regiment of the 'Big Red One', the 1st US Infantry Division, which had held the ridges to the right of the Büllingen-Baugnez road and thus prevented Peiper's follow-up from linking up with him.) Enlisting the aid of another veteran Senator, Charles Potter, who had lost both his legs just after the Ardennes offensive, Eisenhower set in motion the process which would finally bring about the downfall of Joseph McCarthy.

The Watkins Committee officially censured McCarthy, although the latter defended himself with a flood of invective which made a future president of the USA, Lyndon Johnson (no slouch himself when it came to using a four-letter word) describe as 'Not belonging in the Journal of the Senate, but would be more fittingly inscribed on the wall of a men's room. If we sanction this abuse, the Senate may as well close up shop.' It was the Wisconsin senator's swansong. He took to even heavier drinking and died an unlamented early death.

Peiper took note of his benefactor's passing as yet another year went by and he remained incarcerated in Landsberg. In 1954 his former comrade-in-arms and fellow war criminal, General Kurt Meyer, was released from prison and became a leading light in the *HIAG*, the Old Comrades' Association of the *Waffen SS*. General Lammerding, the former commander of the 2nd SS Panzer Division, sentenced to death *in absentia* by a French court for his role in the Oradour massacre, began in that same year his successful career as a building contractor in Dusseldorf. And still Peiper languished in prison, feeling himself forgotten by this new Germany, so full of the success of her 'economic miracle', the 'hard D-Mark', and her new esteem in the eyes of her European neighbours, a country which now believed herself to have replaced Britain in the role of America's most trusted ally. Yet that 'special relationship' between the two countries still could not help to free Peiper.

For once he was wrong. During the third week of December, 1956, he learned that the parole board had unanimously agreed to free him. In the new year he would be released on parole to the town of his choice, Stuttgart, where he would have to report to the local police monthly and not leave the confines of the town without first having permission to do so.

It was all over at last. After thirteen years in jail he was a free man once more. But unknown to the pale, skinny, forty-three year old now emerging into a strange, uncertain civilian world which he had abandoned at the age of twenty to join the *Leibstandarte*, he was now to be faced with a new ordeal. He had served his time, but the world outside was not yet prepared to forgive and forget ex-*Obersturmbannführer* Jochen Peiper.

TWO

'When my father was released,' his daughter Elke remembered many years later, 'he came back to a family in which mother and half-grown children already formed a firm community. Papa was known to us solely through letters and the occasional visit to Landsberg. It wasn't easy to become accustomed to him and it took some time before he was finally accepted really into the family community.'

But it was not only within the family that Peiper experienced difficulties. Gerd Bremer, now building up a prosperous business in Spain, was one of the first of his old pre-war comrades to visit him after his release from prison. He found Peiper 'overly quiet and withdrawn. Physically he looked all right, but the prison years had left their impression. I said to him, trying to shake him out of his apathy, "Jochen, pull yourself together! Get out into the world and find yourself a job."'

In the end Peiper did that. 'I decided to get on the steeplechase for money,' he said years later to the author. But at first there was precious little money to be found in the steeplechase; for he started right at the bottom, *washing cars*! But his energy and intelligence started to pay dividends. Slowly he began to advance up the ladder of promotion. Things were different in peacetime and Peiper's particular kind of ruthlessness and dash were no longer called for in the fat new prosperous Germany of the economic miracle. Still, he moved upwards slowly from blue-collar to white-collar worker. He became publicity manager of the same company that had once manufactured his Panthers – Porsche. But when it was decided to promote him to a higher post, the works council which has to be consulted in such cases, objected. They maintained that a firm whose expensive sports cars went mainly to the United States, could not afford to have a convicted war criminal in a senior post. Peiper had to go.

He left Porsche to join Volkswagen. Here he became sales promotion manager and adviser to its dealer network. He lasted in Wolfsburg for a few years until his past caught up with him once again. Someone in Northern Italy had chanced upon the best-selling account of the Battle of the Bulge, *Battle*, written by American author John Toland. The book contained a picture of Peiper and remarked that he was still alive. As the unknown Italian reader saw it, Peiper was not only responsible for the massacre at Baugnez, but also for the massacre of some of his fellow countrymen at Boves. The Italian alerted the local authorities. In Austria the famous Nazi-hunter, Simon Wiesenthal, took up the case, as did Robert Kempner in Germany, where he had once been one of the US prosecutors at the Nuremberg Trials. The Italian government demanded Peiper's extradition. It was starting all over again.

In Stuttgart, to which he had been paroled, the public prosecutor's office began an investigation, charging Peiper with having 'destroyed the place (the village of Boves) and caused the death of thirty-four villagers'.

'It was no massacre, but a fair fight. War is war,' Peiper protested to the Stuttgart lawyers. But his reputation was against him. For four years the threat of another Dachau trial hung over him. The *Rektor* of the local grammar school refused to accept Peiper's fourteen-year-old son because he objected to schooling 'the son of a murderer and war criminal'. Poor Heinrich, who one day would leave Germany embittered and make a new life for himself in the States, was forced to go elsewhere. An old comrade, a battalion surgeon, for whom Peiper 'would have thrust both hands into the fire', refused to testify in Peiper's defence. He had built up a flourishing practice and he didn't want his patients to know that he had once belonged to the SS; he was finished with that 'old business' for good. All along the line Peiper found himself let down by old friends who dropped him when the new charges were levelled against him.

In the end 112 members of his former battalion and seventeen Italians were heard by the Stuttgart court. In December, 1968, the local public prosecutor decided to drop the case against Peiper for lack of evidence and the fact that 'since that time twenty-five years have passed and it is impossible to clarify what transpired at Boves'. The same thing had happened as at Malmédy. It was Peiper's fate that he could never prove his innocence, just as it was the dilemma of his opponents that they could never prove he had committed a crime.

At Wolfsburg, with that 'not proven' verdict hanging over his head, the many Italian 'guest-workers' employed in the factory protested at Peiper's further employment. Again he had to go but managed to find work in the Stuttgart office of the well-known German magazine and book publishing firm, *Auto, Motor und Sport Verlag*.

By now he was a very bitter man. He knew his past would always be held against him; it would never be forgotten. He knew, too, that he could place no reliance on the new German state and its prosperous, self-satisfied citizens. Privately he called the *Bundesrepublik* a 'bankrupt society' and started to make plans to leave it for good. In 1969 he purchased a small plot of land in eastern France near the little village of Traves, twelve kilometres west of Vesoul. Peiper was preparing himself for self-imposed exile.

In 1970 he was approaching sixty. He was obliged to wear glasses for reading and his hair was grey, plastered down in the style of the thirties. Yet he was still slim and fit, unlike most of his fellow employees in the *Auto, Motor und Sport's* high-rise office block in the centre of Stuttgart. His speech was harsh, quick and bitter, full of outdated wartime soldiers' slang. Acid and cynical about the values of his fellow citizens in the comfortable Swabian capital, he once told the author that he would have liked to drag the last existing tank of his from La Gleize (where it remained as wreck after the battle) and place it at the entrance to the publisher's office block overnight, just to see the look on their 'fat, smug, stupid faces' when they came to work the next morning.

'He had good reason to have lost his faith in his fellow human beings,' his daughter wrote long afterwards. It is not surprising after what he had been through. In spite of his tough talk, Peiper was a broken man. For nearly a quarter of a century he had known nothing but suffering, betrayal and disappointment; little happiness had been granted him. There was no future for him in West Germany and he knew it. Sooner or later his many enemies, who could not forgive him for having escaped the sentence of death imposed upon him at Dachau, would find some means of punishing him again.

Just before he left for good, he told the author with an air of bitter resignation, 'I'm sitting on a powder barrel. Ellis, Kempner and Wiesenthal, they've all tried to get me in the past. One day someone will come along with another "story" and the powder-keg will explode under me. Then it will be all over.'

Little did he know when he made that statement just how true it would prove to be.

THREE

In 1972 Peiper left Germany for good, having had a little wooden house built by the river at Traves. He had been granted a five-year EEC residential permit by the regional Prefecture (in the full knowledge of his identity and reputation). So he went with his long-suffering Sigurd and his two dogs, Timm and Tamm, turning his back on the country for which he had fought for six years and suffered for a further twenty-five. There was no one in particular, save his children, to see him off.

'The only people I took my leave from,' he said later, 'was the tax-office and the only gap I left behind was the garden dwarf I removed from the vase of flowers in my office.' Dropping his cynicism for a moment, he confided to one of his few friends, who reported his sentiments later, that he hoped that one day he and his wife would stand like 'a double oak on the bank of a river, unharmed by the failure of our society and economy which is bound to come'.

Traves consisted of one main street with two shops, an inn, and a rather large church for its population of 300-odd souls, located on a hill in the centre of the village. Peiper and his wife settled down in his modest house on the side of the River Saône, surrounded by a large wall which gained the house the nickname of the 'Fortress' from the locals. The house number was thirteen, but Peiper never had been superstitious and most of his adult life he had had bad luck anyway.

They led a relatively quiet life, living on his meagre service pension, supplemented by what he could earn by translating military history books. About a hundred yards away from Peiper's house there was another owned by a German, a much larger, Bavarian-style structure. The Peipers were friendly with the Germans who lived there, but on the whole they kept to themselves. The villagers, for their part, called him *L'Allemand* and found him to be retiring and quiet. As the burgomaster would say later: 'Everybody knew him and knew what he had been. But he didn't do any harm to anyone.'

At first Sigurd Peiper did not like Traves. As she wrote to her son just before her death, 'The move, the different way of life, a strange new existence, these were all a radical change for me. But as the months passed I grew more and more accustomed to Traves. The inner ballast which I had carried with me for so long fell off as I rediscovered nature. Pa (Peiper) and I became so happy and carefree, making plans for the future, enjoying every new day. I had found my old Jochen again and now it was our innermost wish to end our life there like Philemon and Baucis. Those years in Traves were the happiest of our whole life together because it was there that Pa had times where he was really happy and I with him.'

Peiper enjoyed his dogs, his woods, his music, even his work, though, as he wrote to his son in the mid-seventies: 'The material is depressing really. It is clear to me that these relapses into barbarity took place not just under Hitler, but have happened always. It is the human being who is at fault. He has always attempted to kill his neighbours in order to ensure the survival of himself and his family. Survival of the fittest! . . .The fruit of this realization is resignation.'

At night he would sit in front of his crackling wood fire, smoking his favourite 'Lincoln' tobacco, drinking his 'Earl Grey' tea and listening to classical music. But his mind was always with the past. As he wrote to his son, 'Even here one can never rid oneself of the invisible chains which one drags with one always'.

What did he see in those blazing flames, as the wind whistled through the trees softly outside? What did he hear? Was it the tunes of glory long past? That harsh crunch of hundreds of steel-shod boots stamping down Berlin's *Ost-West Allee* as the bands blared out that spine-chilling, brassy marching music and the crowds cheered those brave young giants in their black uniforms? Or was it the rattle of tank tracks down some nameless road across the steppe, the sun a blood-red ball on the burning horizon, eyes and ears tensed, waiting for that first harsh dry crack which would indicate that the life-and-death struggle had begun yet once again? Was it perhaps the clink of glasses, the lively chatter, the jokes, the *Tanzmusik* of the *Offiziers-kasino*, surrounded by those familiar friendly faces of his comrades; Witt, Panzermeyer, Bremer and all the rest; young men then, now dead or in exile these many years? What went on those long lonely nights in that remote place as he brooded about that old world and what might have been? What voices did he hear, what sights did he see, what old dreams did he dream yet once again?

'So *we beat on, boats against the current, borne back ceaselessly into the past.*'

FOUR

Ever since the start of the special relationship between Bonn and Paris initiated by Konrad Adenauer, Chancellor of the Federal Republic, and Charles de Gaulle, President of France, back in the fifties, the East has made determined efforts to destabilize that relationship. In particular, the East German Ministry of State Security, first under the command of party bully-boy Erick Mielke, and later under the much more sophisticated leadership of General Wolf, has played an important role in supplying communist parties and fellow travellers in the West with the details of the crimes of German war criminals. The aim was, and has always been, to make it clear to France that West Germany is the haven of those Germans who did so much harm to France during the Occupation and who even today are still revanchists, determined to restore the 'New Order', even if it is only by means of the 'economic miracle' and the common market. The Nazi past, so East Berlin reasons, must be put to use to destroy any real rapprochement between France and West Germany. Thus in 1953 the East Germans supplied Paris with the information needed to convict those of the 2nd SS Panzer Division in French hands of the massacre at Oradour. Six days later it was discovered that fourteen of the convicted SS men were *French citizens* – Alsatians who had joined the SS. Hastily the National Assembly met and decided to free the Alsatian murderers. One of the deputies who voted for their release was Deputy François Mitterand. Thirty years later, as President of France, he visited the abandoned village of Oradour, but the streets remained empty. The locals had long memories and boycotted the President's visit.

In 1962 the East again attempted to have the Oradour massacre case re-opened in order to have those officers, including General

Lammerding, who had been sentenced to death *in absentia*, tried.
But that particular attempt to sour Franco-German relations failed
and it is only as I write that East Berlin has finally managed to have one
of the 'Oradour criminals', an insignificant 62-year-old former SS
Untersturmführer, Heinz Barth, put on trial.

Undoubtedly the specialists in East Berlin's office of disinformation
will have a field day when Klaus Barbie is brought to trial, showing his
links not only with US Intelligence, but also with West Germany's own
intelligence service, the *Bundesnachrichtendienst*. Again the French
will be shown what strange bedfellows they had landed themselves
with in Bonn.

Thus it was that when that nosy ironmonger of Vesoul telephoned
Paris with his startling information that a well-known and convicted
Nazi war criminal was living in France, the Party sensed its opportunity. For some time the French Communist Party had been agitating
strongly against the cosy Franco-German relationship. Now they had
a perfect opportunity to destabilize that friendship. East Berlin was
appealed to.

The information the communists needed was not long in coming.

On 21 July, 1976, militant communists appeared in Traves and
began handing out leaflets, stating: 'A war criminal lives among you,
an SS man. *Peiper out!*' Overnight great white swastikas were smeared
on the village walls and the street leading to Peiper's house. The
burgomaster, M. Rigoulot, began receiving 'phone calls demanding
that he should send Peiper away, otherwise he would be murdered.
In Vesoul public demonstrations were held against *L'Allemand*.

Peiper himself began to receive anonymous 'phone calls, threatening: 'We'll set your house on fire. On 14 July, we'll murder you!'

Peiper remained calm. He told a reporter from the local paper: 'I've
lived here six happy years. That's a lot in one lifetime. I live quietly and
at peace here and would like to continue doing so.'

The threats turned to violence and by now Peiper knew that his
letters were being opened by communists in the service of the French
Post Office and his telephone calls were being overheard. But he did
not weaken. When, however, he read in the papers of a conference
held in a hotel in Paris's Place de l'Opera where eight hooded men
swore that they were going to kill him and his kind, he decided to
appeal for help. But Peiper was a political embarrassment to both the
French and German authorities. Neither the French *gendarmerie* nor
the West German Embassy in Paris seemed interested in the fate of the
ex-war criminal.

On 21 June, 1976, the communist newspaper *L'Humanité*, giving

East Berlin as the source of its information, published a full account of Peiper's past. After Peiper's death its leader writer wept crocodile tears and maintained that 'every assassination is absurd and bad', though in the end he reverted to the paper's original tone and said, 'Peiper is the most criminal of all criminals ever executed in France'.

The *Humanité* article made the ball roll even faster. It was followed by other articles, some fairly accurate, others embellished or distorted. Peiper was mentioned in the same breath as those 'writing-desk murderers', Himmler and Eichmann. In the furore, as June gave way to July, much political capital was made out of the fact that Peiper had been given 'sanctuary in France', as if the government in Paris was deliberately harbouring a known Nazi war criminal. It was decided that his *permit de sejour*, which was valid until 22 February, 1977, would not then be renewed. He would have to return to the 'bankrupt republic'.

Peiper had never learned when it was wiser to run away and fight another day, so he dug his heels in and wrote to a friend. 'Overnight my peaceful oasis has become a besieged position. But I shall defend it to the bitter end.'

The tension was rising. Time was running out. Sixty-one now, his face still handsome though furrowed with the lines of harsh experience, Peiper decided to send his wife to Munich, where she would be safe. Thus they parted. He never saw her again.

Peiper remained behind with his dogs, a hunting rifle and an old-fashioned American revolver that someone had loaned him. He was not going to bow down to the communist threat. On 12 July he wrote to another friend in Germany, 'I've just received another ultimatum from the Red Brigade. They're going to put a red cock on the roof of my house. I'd prefer it if they would wait till autumn. By then my wife will be back in Munich and I can arrange a move to Bavaria in peace.'

But his killers were prepared to wait no longer.

FIVE

On Bastille Day 1976, the temperatures in France soared into the high eighties. In Paris the khaki uniforms of the soldiers parading before the President were black with sweat. On the *Autoroute* through Burgundy it was so hot that the sweating tourists heading south drove their boiling-hot cars in their underwear and bikinis. In Normandy pigs died of heatstroke. The Seine had a temperature of eighty-two degrees. Around Traves the meadows were parched a deep brown and the farmers, devoid of foodstuffs, were forced to feed their hungry animals bananas from Guadeloupe.

But, in spite of the heat, the French celebrated their national day as they had always celebrated it, with parades, speeches, fireworks, dancing in the streets and much wine.

For Peiper the day on which he was to be murdered passed peacefully enough. As it began to grow dark and the oppressive heat of the day started to lessen, he went to call on a neighbour with whom he stayed for a while, having turned down the offer of some friends to come and stay with him. Unknown to Peiper, a friendly gendarme, who had advised him to buy a shotgun for his protection, was watching over him. Time passed and nothing happened so he decided to go home.

Silence began to descend upon Traves. The locals were mainly farmers. Bastille Day it might well be, but on the morrow they would have to be out early, feeding their animals and one by one the lights in the village began to go out. Peiper walked back to his house to find that another neighbour, Erwin Ketelhut, a German sculptor, had come to visit him.

'He was absolutely calm and at ease,' Ketelhut, the last man to see him alive, reported later. 'I offered to stay and help him, but he refused. His last words to me were, "I won't be bullied! They can shoot me if they wish, but I'm not going to allow them to beat me into a cripple. If they come, I'm going to defend my home".'

Soon Ketelhut rose to leave; they shook hands German-fashion, wished each other '*Gute Nacht*' and Ketelhut went out into the night, leaving Peiper alone. Soon it would be Thursday, 15 July, and he was still alive. They weren't coming after all.

Shortly after midnight, loud noises woke some of the villagers. Most of them stirred uneasily in their beds and then went back to sleep, probably thinking that some drunken reveller was still letting off fireworks. A few recognized the noise for what it was, gunfire, but they kept that knowledge to themselves.

Two hours later, at 2.30 am, a passing motorist raised the alarm. He had spotted flames coming from the direction of the woods. The timber out there was bone-dry due to the drought and the heat. A forest fire could present a danger for the whole village. The heavy-headed voluntary fire brigade stumbled out of their beds. Hastily the half-dressed men crossed the fields that separated the village from Peiper's house and began to set up their pumps, but nothing happened. Later, some said the brigade's hoses had been deliberately slashed; others said that the delay was simply due to poor maintenance of the equipment. But, whatever the reason, while the firemen cursed and fumbled, trying to get their hoses and pumps to operate, Number Thirteen burned and burned, a bright-red funeral pyre for that lone Black Guard who had not turned and run, but had fought to the last.

'When one regards the tragic, unhappy, and spoiled life of this man,' one of his few friends said later, 'then one can only make a single cold-hearted comment: *Jochen Peiper should have blown his brains out in 1945!*'

Next morning detectives from Vesoul, poking around in the smouldering ruin of No 13, came to the conclusion that the fire had been started by a petrol bomb thrown through the ground-floor window. Peiper's dogs had disappeared (later one of them was found wounded by a bullet fired by the unknown attackers). Peiper himself had gone, too; all that the detectives found inside the wreckage was a charred mess which had once been human, but which was now shrunken by the intense heat to a length of exactly sixty centimetres.

Next to it was Peiper's watch, the American revolver and thirteen boxes of exploded ammunition. Outside, the rifle was found and traces of bullets fired from it were discovered among the trees. A little further away a drawer full of documents was discovered, plus an unexploded incendiary device attached to a tree.

As the detectives reconstructed the events of that night, they concluded that the unknown assailants had thrown two Molotov cocktails at the house. Being mainly of wood, it had gone up in flames immediately. Peiper had continued to fire at his attackers until they fled. But the floor of the first storey had collapsed beneath him and that had been that. *But was the corpse that of Jochen Peiper?*

Neither his widow nor the three French specialists brought from Paris could establish that fact with any certainty. So a section of the lower jaw was taken from the charred torso to be sent to Munich, where Peiper's dentist would examine it and, in due course, give his verdict. Meanwhile tension mounted in Traves. Menacing telephone calls were received in Vesoul and in Traves, threatening reprisals. The village fête, held annually in August, was cancelled. Naturally, the Press had a field day. The more sensational papers in the USA and Great Britain informed their readers that Peiper had escaped after killing one of his assailants, whose charred corpse the detectives had found in the wrecked house. *Obersturmbannführer* Peiper had gone underground for good, like some latter-day Martin Bormann. Already he might well be on his way to South America to disappear into some remote Bolivian jungle. Peiper was said to have been 'liquidated' by East Berlin's Ministry of State Security in order to sour relations between France and West Germany. Another story had it that the Baader-Meinhoff terrorist gang had got him.

In France, however, the Press generally took the body to be that of Peiper. With the exception of the communist papers, they denounced the brutal murder. Many former members of the French Resistance expressed their disgust at the killing. Even Beate Klarsfeld, the German woman married to a French Jew who had long been the *bête noire* of Germany's ex-Nazis (once she had even struck a West German chancellor across the face because he had belonged to the Nazi Party) stated that, 'A man who paid for his crimes with twelve years in jail has nothing more to account for'.

The local *curé* of Traves, Monsieur Ducros, to whose faith Peiper did not belong, prepared a statement for French TV in which he said, 'I deplore the murder of Peiper and blame communist propaganda for the whole business'. French TV dared not broadcast the priest's statement and he, in his turn, was threatened with death by anonymous telephone callers. This did not shake his resolve. In another interview with a local paper, he said, 'I will pray for him (Peiper) and his murderers, but the peace of our village is destroyed for good'.

Meanwhile the police had been half-heartedly investigating the murder. Several youngsters were questioned, especially those suspected to being involved in breaking open Peiper's letter box at No 13, a matter which Peiper had not reported to the police. One of these youngsters did in fact confess to having started the fire. A little later he retracted his confession and the French police dropped the charge against him, as the self-confessed arsonist was known to be psychologically unstable and it was generally accepted that his confession had its origins in the emotional atmosphere that pervaded the area.

In the end, Peiper's Munich dentist identified the jaw as belonging to Jochen Peiper. The teeth sent from Traves fitted those on Peiper's dental records in his office. The corpse was officially declared to be that of Peiper.

Nearly ten years have passed since 14 July, 1976, but the mystery of Jochen Peiper's death remains unsolved. Was the attack that hot Bastille Day an attempt at intimidation which resulted in an unintentional death? Or was it a deliberate murder, timed to take place on France's most important public holiday in order to gain the maximum publicity? We do not know. Since that time the French police have quietly let the case drop; they have made no further attempts to trace the culprits, who undoubtedly were local. Nor has the West German government put any pressure on the French authorities to do anything about the unsolved murder of one of its citizens. For both parties Peiper was and is a political embarrassment.

In the end the corpse was transferred to Germany where it was interred in the family tomb at Schondorf am Ammersee, Bavaria, whence his wife would follow him three years later. In 1976, however, she wrote to her son, now as bitter at the reaction of the West German public and media to his father's death as once Peiper himself had been (soon he, too, would go into self-imposed exile in the United States), 'Whatever happened that terrible night no longer matters. Pa would not and could not have left Traves. If he had been able to see Traves, his dream of peace and happiness, in its present state, life wouldn't have seemed worth living; his heart would have been broken. So Pa is at peace. No one any more can hurt or torture his spirit. I will never sell Traves.'

Today, seven years after Sigurd Peiper's early death, that plot of land near Traves is still unsold. At her funeral on 17 April, 1979, her son solemnly swore, '*Mami und Papi*, we will never sell Traves'.

Now the forest has almost reclaimed the abandoned site, but inside the ruined house there are still the charred chairs on which Peiper smoked his old pipe and listened to his records. Outside, too, there are traces of his passing. The woodshed, still piled high with logs from the wood where, 'I work horrors with axe and motor saw,' as he wrote to his son, 'and make a mess of Mother Nature'. The two heaps of blackened refuse still lie outside the door, where the police back in 1976 sifted the charred contents for clues. There are even bottles of preserves made by Sigurd Peiper in the cellar.

Today there is an eerie feeling about the place. One strains one's eyes and ears, trying to catch the sight and sound of anyone approaching through the trees and it is a relief to leave the ruined house, get into the car and drive away, leaving Traves and its watching eyes behind. Could the murderers still be there in that straggle of houses running up the hill towards the church? Might the lone farmer in his 'work-blue', leading his cow down the third-class road running out of the place, be one of them? It is good to be gone from that eerie place, where Peiper fought his last battle.

He had been threatened with death many times, but he was incapable of running away from danger; he had always been like that. His inability to be a coward, or even sensible about threats, had taken him into the firing line for the last time and the manner of his dying was unfair and absurd.

Yet there is something tragic, perhaps even a little noble, about the way the skinny, white-haired old man, alone in a foreign country, fought off his enemies that July night. It might have been the kind of death that *Obersturmbannführer* Jochen Peiper, the last commander of the premier regiment of the premier division of the *Waffen SS*, would have picked for himself, *with a weapon in his hands.*

ENVOI

Long after his capture by Jochen Peiper, the then First Lieutenant (now Dr) L. Bouck, who saw the SS Colonel only once, in the Café Palm, wrote to the latter, 'I know you faced charges of having your men shoot prisoners-of- war at Honsfeld, Büllingen and Malmédy. Because we were not molested after a day of severe battle with the best German troops, I have always thought you had been accused of something over which you had no control. It is well known that in the heat of battle tempers flare and men will do things they normally would not do. Many situations like this happened with our own troops.'*

Dr Bouck's letter to Peiper was perhaps the only tribute that the latter was ever to receive from one of the men who had fought against him that December, perhaps indeed the only acknowledgement that Peiper ever carried out that brave dash for the River Meuse. At every turn on the route each skirmish is marked with a weathering stone dedicated to the victorious dead. Each summer old men, Belgian and American, come to pay their respects to those who were once their comrades when they were young.

Naturally there are no monuments to *Kampfgruppe* Peiper, unless one counts the dead Americans at the Baugnez crossroads. Ironically, Peiper never saw the crossroads which later proved so fatal to him, though elsewhere there are traces of his passing: the bullet holes in the rough, white-painted houses in the hamlet of Lanzerath; the Café Palm, where Bouck saw Peiper, still virtually the same as it was when Peiper flung open the door and thought the war had gone to sleep; bomb craters on the heights above Stavelot where American dive-bombers wreaked havoc with Peiper's stalled column; the still shattered trees along the Amblève valley where the deadly American

* Letter in the author's possession.

artillery fire stopped Major Knittel's reconnaissance battalion dead. There, if you wander off the main road into the forest, you can still find a rusting rifle clip or an ammunition box date-stamped '1944', some rotted webbing and the occasional grey belt buckle with the faded legend engraved upon it '*Gott mit uns*' (God with us). The traces are there and the forests are still heavy with the imagined presence of those frightened young men, American and German, who once fought and died there.

But there is nothing imaginary about what confronts you when you swing off the main road through La Gleize where it all ended. Turn towards the little square and the rebuilt church and there it is, its long 88 mm cannon pointing straight at your car: Peiper's last tank, looking as powerful and as sinister as that grey snowy day over forty years ago when it had first rumbled over the Belgian border and it had all started.

APPENDIX

The Arrest of Jochen Peiper

The search for the 'Malmedy Criminals' started almost at once. Allied investigators began their enquiries straight after the frozen bodies of the dead were dug up at Baugnez in the third week of January, 1945. The Belgian 'Prince Regent's War Crimes Inquiry' soon turned up witnesses among local civilians who identified Peiper's Battle Group. German POWs, currying favour or frightened that they might be accused themselves, added their testimony to that of the civilians of the Ambleve Valley.*

The search spread to France and then to Britain. What had happened in Baugnez was now classified officially as a 'war crime' by the US 1st Army's Inspector General's Branch. It concluded, after examining the bodies, that there was definite evidence of the murder of 'approximately 120 American POWs'. So no expense was spared and in a remote English provincial town, while the war still raged at the front, the inquiry's first official hearing took place.

The town was the genteel English spa town of Harrogate, never bombed, untouched by war save for the influx of London civil servants evacuated there years before and the US military hospital set up in early '44 in a former independent girls' school (long since demolished). Here three officers, British, American and Canadian, questioned Staff Sergeant Henry Zach, who had feigned death in the field outside the Cafe Bodarwé, now burned to the ground. He was followed by several other 'survivors', as they were now being called.

---

* A quarter of a century later, when the author took up the same trail, it was clear to him that the civilians questioned in 1945 had in some cases saved their own skins by being quite economical with the truth.

In March, 1945, the court of inquiry submitted its findings. They concluded that it was 'beyond question that seventy-two unarmed prisoners' had been murdered. They stated unequivocally that the murder had been 'unprovoked, deliberate and brutal'.

In Washington, in the meantime, the authorities wondered what they should do about the incident now known officially as the 'Malmédy Massacre'. The war was still being fought in Europe and the US Army was facing some tough, even brutal, fighting on the other side of the Rhine. Indeed there had been an unfortunate incident in Patton's Third Army, when one of his divisions, incited by an unfounded rumour, had deliberately killed some 500 SS men taken prisoner from the German 6th SS Mountain Division. But the public had already gained wind of the Malmédy incident. Indeed the matter had been brought to the notice of the ailing President Roosevelt himself (he wasn't particularly moved by it). In the end the US War and Justice Departments submitted a formal memorandum on war crimes in general to the President. It included a commitment to an international trial and to prosecuting even pre-war atrocities dating back to 1933. These, the departments' lawyers admitted, were neither war crimes in the technical sense nor crimes against international law. However, they were justified because 'The declared policy of the United Nations is that these crimes, too, shall be punished; and the interests of postwar security and a necessary rehabilitation of the German people, as well as the demands of justice, required this to be done.'

In other words, if one overlooks the sop to 'necessary rehabilitation of the German people', the US authorities wer going to do what they liked, whether or not their actions had any basis in international law. Things, indeed, looked very black for *Obersturmführer* Jochen Peiper and the 800 survivors of the 'Fürhrers' Fire Brigade', *Kampfgruppe Peiper*.

But where was Peiper?

After the near panic-stricken scramble of the Ist SS to cross the Austrian River Enns, the demarcation line between the US Army to the West and the Red Army to the East, many of the exhausted, beaten SS man were only too glad to surrender to the Americans. At least in American hands they'd be safe from what they regarded as the 'bestialities' of the 'Ivans'. Some of their senior officers refused to surrender, unlike their divisional commander, General Kumms, who did. Peiper's friend *Obersturmbannführer* Max Hansen dressed himself in his best uniform, complete with

Knight's Cross, and set off into an uncertain future, openly and proudly displaying the fact that he was an SS officer. He didn't get far. Others, like acting *Standartenführer* Frey, Peiper's pre-war company commander, adopted a much lower profile. Although he was nearly six foot three and his face was scarred so that he looked like a caricature of the typical Prussian officer of anti-German legend, he made his way right through France, into Spain and thence to South America, pretending to be an American soldier, though he spoke barely a word of English. Presumably his appearance ensured that no one would have dared to stop him – certainly not the author, who met Herr Frey when he was an old man. Even then he looked a tough nut.

Peiper and a few of his comrades decided to go it alone. He hated to abandon the division, but he knew what his fate would be if the allies handed him over to the Russians, which he suspected they would. He headed for home and his wife in Bavaria, whom he hadn't seen for nearly six months. But he didn't make it. He was captured, according to his own statement, some six miles away from 'my objective'. And that was that.

Most of the men of the Ist SS Division were still in camps – 'hunger camps', they called them – in Austria. But Peiper was thrown in a huge POW camp just outside Nuremberg, where the Nazi Party had held their annual rallies. Now it was a bombed and blasted wreck after the US 7th Army had fought for the medieval city for nearly a week.

Here, under the command of Lieutenant-Colonel Henry 'Red' Clisson, a tough infantryman who still proudly wore the red patch of his old division 'the Big Red One', America's premier infantry division, the First, 75,000 SS men from both the *Waffen SS* and the *'Totenkopf'* (Death's Head), which had supplied concentration camp guards, were interned.

But, as one of the guards from US Intelligence, of Belgian nationality, explained later, 'It was a dangerous camp to be in. Nightly there were murders and kangaroo courts in which "traitors" were sentenced to death [usually by drowning in the latrines]. Even those of us who were armed never felt really secure in the camp. We slept *inside* the place in old *Wehrmacht* huts and we had to be on our guard twenty-four hours a day. Finally it got too dangerous and we asked to be transferred to outside the wire.'

All the same, working 'in clouds of the insecticide DDT', the interrogators from the US Corps of Counter-Intelligence tried to sort out the sheep from the goats. Their technique, in part, was relatively crude and simple, but it seemed to work. One of the CIC agents, who spoke German, had groups of POWs to be checked marched to one of the few remaining buildings, where he gave them a free movie show. But the films that Agent John Centner showed the SS men could be hardly described as entertainment.

They were films taken in German concentration camps such as Belsen, Dachau and Natzweiler in France, just after the British and Americans had liberated them, plus Russian films (not so well received)* of German cities after they had been taken by the Red Army. While the silent films ran to audiences of up to 2,000 stubborn SS men, John Centner would comment, 'This is what you are being accused of. Once we identify the guilty ones, those of you who are not guilty will be released. So if you have any information or know anything about these atrocities please tell us. If you're not guilty that will help you get out of here a lot faster.'

Not that all of the SS POWs were that eager to escape. Each day many thousands of them were sent to Nuremberg to clean up the destruction. As the Belgian CIC agent explained, 'They were not too eager to run away. One day one of them did. That night the escapee was back, knocking on the camp gate, asking to be let in. He explained that he had gone to visit his girlfriend. Now he was wanting back. In the city there weren't three meals a day. Conditions outside were not as good as they were in our camp.'

By now the counter-intelligence agents working in the POW camps had been ordered to keep a sharp lookout for the 'chief organizer of the Malmédy Massacre'.

Thus it was that, thumbing his way through the complete card index on the camp's inmates, the Belgian CIC agent 'spotted the name of Joachim (or Jochen)** Peiper of the Ist SS Panzer. . . . He was a legend to us, a superhuman combat leader. Now here was his 3 × 5" card in our file of prisoners. I really got excited and went to see Colonel Clisson, our camp commander.'

But where was Peiper in the huge camp with its shifting POW

---

* According to SS sources, when the Ist SS retook Charkov in 1943, they found their comrades who had been captured by the Red Army had been brutally murdered and stuffed down a well. They thought both sides were equally cruel and savage in the war in Russia.
** He had abandoned the Jewish name of Joachim for the Germanic-sounding Jochen.

population, many of them experienced in dodging head counts, going to ground in the latrines, etc?

Finally a CIC agent Richard C. Lang* found him. Immediately the identification and arrest of Peiper zipped up the channel of command. After all, the order for his arrest had come from no less a person than the Secretary for War himself.

Immediately Clisson was ordered to provide an armed guard to take him to Munich where the War Crimes Commission wanted to see him 'without delay' and there the camp photographer took a last photo of the departing 'guest'. He is looking at a smiling Lang standing outside the command car, is dressed in the black cap of the *Panzerkorps* and a long grey *Wehrmacht* coat. He stands there, with his hands in his pockets in a very unsoldierly posture. Perhaps it was really a gesture of contempt, a half-cynical look on his handsome face. Perhaps he knew what was soon to come. Then he would no longer smile.

The Belgian CIC agent, who was to drive the command car to Munich, was not too happy about the arrest. Fifty years later, the Belgian, who had been present with Lang at the liberation of several concentration camps and was no friend of the Germans, said, 'My personal feeling was that it was not Peiper himself who ordered the massacre in Baugnez.'

But feelings were no longer important. Peiper was entering the world stage. Hereafter for another three decades he would never be freed from what had happened at Malmédy. Presidents of the USA would attack him, Popes and Prelates would defend him. To no avail. In the end it would be the bullet of an unknown assassin which would finally solve the puzzle of the 'Malmédy Massacre' and give him the peace he craved.

---

* Still alive aged 89 at the time of writing.

INDEX

Anderson, Colonel, 73
Antwerp, 44–5

Baldwin, Senator, 156, 159, 160–1
Baugnez, 59, 61, 66–67, 95, 102, 121, 137, 145, 169, 185
Berger, General Gottlob, 8
Berlin, 6
Boves, 26–7, 172
Bremer, Gerd, 16, 171
Brodel, Johann, 55–6
Büllingen, 47, 55, 57, 141, 145

Chapin, Corporal, 75
Clay, General, 153–4, 156
Currie, Major, 36

Dachau, 9, 129, 137, 145, 151–2, 156, 161
Dalbey, Brigadier-General Josiah, 130, 145, 149, 150
Dietrich, General (Joseph) 'Sepp', (x), 7, 14–15, 21, 35, 38–9, 85, 108, 117, 123–4, 130, 132, 147, 150
Dinse, Captain, 26

Ellis, Lieutenant-Colonel Burton F., 111–12, 121, 125–6, 130–6, 138–141, 147, 151, 160–1, 173
Engel, Colonel Gerhard, 47, 49
Everett, Jr., Colonel Willis M., 130, 133, 135–8, 140–1, 143, 145, 149, 150–151, 153, 155, 162

Falaise, 35
Fleps, Private Georg, 104, 106, 146
Ford, Private Homer, 61–4, 105
Friedrichs, Corporal Heinz, 114–15

Goebbels, Josef, 82
Gregoire, Madame Regine, 78–9, 80, 95, 98, 121, 134–5

Hausser, Lieutenant-General Paul, 19, 22–3, 33, 36–7, 167
Hechler, Major Ken, (x)
Hennecke, Lieutenant, 69, 70
Heydrich, Lina, 12
Himmler, Heinrich, 10–12, 14, 110
Hitler, Adolf, 14, 31, 39, 108, 120–1, 132
Hoffman, Colonel, 50–2

Jodl, Colonel-General, 31–2, 38, 147

Keele, Captain, 62
Kluge, General Hans von, 32, 35
Knittel, Major, 76–7, 101, 103, 150, 186
Kraemer, General Fritz, 117, 123, 124, 130, 143
Kraetschmer, Ernst Gunther, 9

La Gleize, 73–4, 76, 81, 86–8, 90, 95, 99, 122, 138–9, 141, 173, 186
Lammerding, General Heinz, (xii), 178
Lanzerath, 50–1, 53, 55

Lary, Second-Lieutenant Virgil, 61–2, 66, 104–6, 121, 133–4
Lehmann, Rudolf, 29
Le Joly, Henri, 59, 61–3, 122, 141, 146–9
Leopold, King of Belgium, 97

McCarthy, Senator Joseph, 113, 157, 159, 160–2, 169
McCown, Major Hal, 81–3, 87–9, 90–1, 110–11, 138–9, 140
Malmédy, 59, 60–5, 96, 102, 105, 133, 143, 145, 156, 162
Mohnke, General, 43–5, 47, 86, 92
Mueller, Peter, 55–6

Nicolay, Louis, 77

Paris, 5
Patton, General George S., 31, 74, 109, 145
Paul, Mr, 119
Peiper, Elke, 163
Peiper, Jochen:
  Birth, 6
  Education, 7
  Promotions, 10, 14, 19, 43, 107
  Campaigns, 13, 33, 40, 57, 70, 76, 85, 109
  Post-1945, 5 (Crime), 123 (Prison), 124 (Confession), 130 (Trial), 150 (Sentence), 165 (Pardoning), 174 (leaves Germany), 180 (Murder)
Peiper, Sigurd, 12, 153, 163, 175, 182–183

Peiper, Waldemar, 6
Pergrin, Colonel David, 63–6, 98
Perl, William R., 114–17, 119, 122–5, 135–6, 140, 155, 159, 160
Poetschke, Major Werner, 103, 146
Postel, Lieutenant-General Georg, 19, 20–1
Priess, General Hermann, 85–6, 107, 117, 123–4, 130

Roehm, Captain Ernst, 6
Rosenfeld, Colonel, 130, 137–9, 141
Rudel, Colonel Hans-Ulrich, 23–4
Rulien, Major Miles, 141
Rundstedt, Field-Marshal Gerd von, 45, 147

Schumacher, Captain Raphael, 119, 142, 156, 160
Simpson, Judge, 155
Siptrott, Sergeant, 103–4, 146
Stavelot, 68–9, 70, 74–6, 78, 80, 86, 88–9, 98–9, 100
Stuttgart, 172

Timberlake, General, 58
Traves, 4–5, 173–5, 180, 182–3
Trois Ponts, 70–2, 76–8, 135, 145

Vesoul, 173, 178, 181–2

Wiesenthal, Simon, 172–3
Wisch, General Theodor, 33

Zwigart, Private, 139